History of the
UNITED STATES II

CLEP* Test Study Guide

All rights reserved. This Study Guide, Book and Flashcards are protected under the US Copyright Law. No part of this book or study guide or flashcards may be reproduced, distributed or stored in a retrieval system, or transmitted in any form or by any means, electronic, mechanical, photocopying, recording, or otherwise, without the prior written permission of the publisher Breely Crush Publishing, LLC.

© 2026 Breely Crush Publishing, LLC

*CLEP is a registered trademark of the College Entrance Examination Board which does not endorse this book.

971010420143

Copyright ©2003 - 2026, Breely Crush Publishing, LLC.

All rights reserved.

This Study Guide, Book and Flashcards are protected under the US Copyright Law. No part of this publication may be reproduced, distributed or stored in a retrieval system, or transmitted in any form or by any means, electronic, mechanical, photocopying, recording, or otherwise, without the prior written permission of the publisher Breely Crush Publishing, LLC.

Published by Breely Crush Publishing, LLC
10808 River Front Parkway
South Jordan, UT 84095
www.breelycrushpublishing.com

ISBN-10: 1-61433-653-9
ISBN-13: 978-1-61433-653-2

Printed and bound in the United States of America.

*CLEP is a registered trademark of the College Entrance Examination Board which does not endorse this book.

Table of Contents

The Causes and Impacts of Major Wars in U.S. History 1
    1865-1914 (and Prior) 1
The American Civil War 2
    Causes of the War 2
    Social life in America's During the 1800's 2
    Industrialization 3
    Immigration 3
    Religiosity 4
    Standard of Living 4
    Demographics 5
Growing Differences Between the North and South 6
    Slavery as a Southern Institution 6
    Importance of Cotton 7
    Living Condition of Slaves 7
    Abolition Movement 8
    Leaders 9
    Methods and Tactics of Abolition 10
    Uncle Tom's Cabin 10
    Reconstruction Acts 11
    Fourteenth and Fifteenth Amendments 11
    Scalawags and Carpetbaggers 12
The Spanish-American War 12
    Teller Amendment 12
    Filipino Insurrection 12
World War I – 1914-1929 13
World War II – 1939-1945 14
    Rosie Riveter 15
    Double "V" Campaign 15
The Cold War 16
    Dr. Strangelove 16
    Alger Hiss 16
    Hungarian Uprising 17
The Korean and Vietnam War 17
    Gulf of Tonkin Resolution 17
The Results of War 18
The Development of American Political Parties 18
    Other Political Parties 20
Welfare Programs 21
    The New Deal 21
    Social Insurance 21
    Medicare 22
    Public Assistance 22

Constitutional Amendments 23
The Supreme Court 26
    Sacco and Venzetti Trial 34
Political Movements in the United States 35
    Isolationism and Expansionism 36
Demographics and Industry 37
    Demographic Trends 37
    Demographic Variables 37
    Immigrants 37
    Nature of Work 37
    Triangle Shirtwaist Fire 38
    Northern Securities Case 39
    Unions 39
    Common Occupations 40
Social Growth of America 40
    Immigration and the History of Racial Minorities 40
    Freedom Summer of 1964 41
    Urbanization 41
    Growth of Cities 42
    The Changing Nature of Agricultural Life 43
    Economic Growth and Development 44
    Economic Fabric 44
    Industrial Growth 45
    Trends in Women and the Family 46
    Phyllis Schlafly 48
    Emma Goldman 49
    The Boy Scouts 49
    Scopes Trial 49
    C. Wright Mills 50
Major Movements of the Arts 50
    Painting and Sculptures 50
    Literature 52
    Nonfiction Literature 53
    Theater 54
    Film 54
    Architecture 54
Diplomacy and International Relations 55
Sample Test Questions 56
Test Taking Strategies 112
What Your Score Means 112
Test Preparation 113
Legal Note 113

 The Causes and Impacts of Major Wars in U.S. History

1865-1914 (AND PRIOR)

- The New England – New York area had become center stage for the French-English Wars. In the Upper Ohio Valley, French and Indian Wars erupted and the repercussions were felt in Europe. England and France started what is known as the Seven Years War. Quebec in Canada was captured by the English Army in 1759 and in 1760 Montreal had no option but to surrender. In 1763, The Treaty of Paris was signed by England and France. The result was the acquisition French Canada, as well as England taking areas east of Mississippi River. Also, England received Florida from Spain to whom France had surreptitiously ceded it earlier. British supremacy in the brave New World had been established.
- From 1763 to 1789, the relationship between the colonies and the Empire, which was exceedingly friendly and cordial at the beginning, started to turn sour, mainly because of the Empire persisting with their restrictive policies as well as their imposition of direct taxes. The colonies resented the behavior of the Empire and decided that the only way out was independence from the yoke of Great Britain. The British became adamant and brought in the Five Intolerable Acts, in the year 1774. War began in the year 1775 and under the command of George Washington, Colonial forces won the war; on October 1781 Lord Cornwallis of the British Empire had no alternative but to surrender: They declared Independence from the British and the United States was born.
- In 1845 Texas was annexed. This resulted in friction between the United States and Mexico over the demarcation of the boundary separating the two countries. The subsequent declaration of war in May 1846 and the fierce battle that ensued saw the U.S. conquering California, the New Mexico region and Northern Mexico, all of which were later ceded by Mexico.
- In the year 1898, after almost half a century of peace and the reconstruction and rebuilding of the nation, the Spanish American War started. Though the U.S. government was not enthusiastic in declaring war, yet it had no option because of overwhelming public sentiment against Spanish atrocities on the Cuban people, who were silently revolting against Spanish imperialism. The U.S. won the war in no time. As the result, the U.S. received possession of the Spanish colonies in the Philippines and Puerto Rico. It also annexed the Hawaii Islands and Cuba was assured help to set up its own self-government. The United States, which had remained aloof from the rest of the world until then, had become a world power.

 The American Civil War

CAUSES OF THE WAR

The Civil War was caused by a separatist conflict when the eleven Southern slave states declared their secession and intent for the expansion of slavery. The Confederate States of America was formed to back the prospect of the expansion, led by President Jefferson Davis (1808-1889), a former statesman who was President of the Confederate States of America.

It was due to the apprehension of the economic depletion that led these states to put together a plan for the growth and expansion of slavery. Those states depended heavily on the slave labor for their crops, especially cotton. Opponents to slavery were concerned about the expansion of slavery, yet both sides knew that if not for the expansion of slavery it would one day slow down or be eliminated altogether.

The United States Federal Government, the Union, led by Abraham Lincoln (1809-1865) opposed secession and rejected any right for the expansion of slavery. Although slavery was illegal in the Northern states, not all were completely against slavery and only a small number of Northerners actively opposed it.

Prior to the election of Abraham Lincoln an arrival of certain structured events helped in the accumulation of the origins of the American Civil War. The election of Abraham Lincoln was one of the main motivations for the formation of the Confederate States of America, in fear that Lincoln would eventually abolish slavery. Each of those events had a multitude of complex political issues, which included federalism, sectionalism, slavery, expansionism, economics, and modernization with each side, the North and the South, taking a very different approach and opinion to each of these concerns.

SOCIAL LIFE IN AMERICA'S DURING THE 1800'S

Preceding the onset of the Civil War and within the first decade of the 19th century, social lifestyles weren't much different than those of the late 18th century. Women continued to wear long flowing skirts, with a blouse typically featuring a long neckline and a separate half-blouse with a high neckline. Shoes were worn not for comfort, but for style and during those years one shoe could fit both feet.

The schools of this era were governed and financially supplied by the local community with very little statewide supervision. Normally the mothers in the community would choose the teacher, usually a man with very little college education himself. Michigan became the first state to enter a statement that promoted the responsibility of the supervision of the public schools.

INDUSTRIALIZATION

Because of trading embargoes, Congress had little power to tax imports from foreign lands until a Congressional meeting in 1787 gave congress the power to tax imports, regulate international trading, and national trading.

The power Congress had to tax and regulate imports into the country pushed them to offending exporting countries. Threats made by the British and the French countries led to the 1807 Embargo, prohibiting American trade with foreign countries. Although the embargo failed, it did force Americans to begin manufacturing their own goods. The end result was industrialization.

Manual power gave way to factories using machinery first driven by waterpower and eventually by steam power. This aided in the massive amount of small farming towns to grow into industrial cities. Large cities began to grow at an alarming rate, such as New York, Boston, Philadelphia and Baltimore. Canals and railroads that were built, making it easier for trading and access to products from the West.

IMMIGRATION

Immigration had both adverse and beneficial effects on the United States during the 19th century. The majority of immigrants came through the United States during the 1830's. Many immigrants sought out the opportunities of the new country – Ireland and Germany providing a large percentage of immigrants. This was due in part to the poverty felt in Ireland, the potato famine, as well as the crop failures in Germany. Individuals who migrated to the United States during those years sent travel tickets and money to family and relatives in their native land, encouraging them to take the journey to the States.

In the late 1700's to early 1800's an estimated 250,000 immigrants found new opportunities in the new country. The largest group to arrive in the early 1800's was the Scotch Irish, and in the year 1801-1802 as many as 20,000 Irish and German citizens came to the United States as immigrants.

The largest amount of the nation's population in the 1800's settled along the eastern seaboard and had increased nearly thirty percent according to the 1790 census. European immigrants mainly worked in factories, built the railroads of the North, and eventually settled their families in the West.

Immigrants coming into to the United States in the early 1830's were near 600,000 strong, four times the amount that came through the century before. The 1860's saw the biggest hike in the population in the history of the United States, 1,427,337 immigrants mostly settling in Minnesota and Wisconsin.

The constant streams of newcomers led to an opposition to immigration. Americans opposing the onslaught of so many newcomers formed structured organizations and secret societies such as the Order of the United Americans and the Know Nothing Party in protest of the surge.

RELIGIOSITY

Religiosity refers to the aspects of religious activity, dedication and belief. Religion was a major part of all social, educational and business matters throughout the 1800's. Just before the mark of the 19th century the U.S. adopted into its constitution the eradication of church and state ties. The First Amendment reads, "Congress shall make no law respecting an establishment of religion, or prohibiting the free exercise thereof."

The majority of the population of Americans practiced the Protestant religion within the beginning of the nineteenth century; there were only a few scattered Catholics and Jews. It was uncommon during the turn of the century to hear of non-Christian religions such as Islam and Buddhist.

More than one million immigrants came to the U.S. between the years of 1845-1855 from Ireland. The majority of these Irish immigrants were Roman-Catholic; these were the first seen Roman-Catholics to immigrate to the United States. The diversity of Religion continued to increase when predominately Lutheran immigrants from Germany came to the U.S. for salvation from the German uprising of 1848.

Many religious groups came to America to elude persecution or the wickedness of their fellow citizens from their country. The lands and openness of the New Country gave immigrants the ability to establish American denominational churches such as the Church of Jesus Christ of Latter-day Saints, Jehovah's Witness, Christian Science Churches, and the Seventh-day Adventist church. These groups relatively came together with the same religious factors, but outside issues such as slavery and other social, educational and political factors resulted in sectional division.

STANDARD OF LIVING

The Northeast felt an economical decrease in agricultural activity caused mainly from the migration of farmers who settled in the West. New England states such as New York, New Jersey and eastern Pennsylvania felt the effects of this decrease the most. In addition, the shipping and foreign trade industries both were nearly ruined by the economic warfare from the war of 1812.

The 19th century for Western Americans was overwhelmingly rural in its theme, and work was very tough on settlers; they had to clear the lands that were overgrown with forests and debris to form communities and local governments. Life on the frontier was also dangerous; when settlers came in to clear the lands they were meet with hostile Indians. Most settlers were valued more for their capability and enthusiasm to work with their hands rather than their ancestry links or their educational background.

The principles, theories on slavery, economy and social life differed greatly in the South from that of the North. The South's living standards were led by social grace and culture. The Southern slave owners were left with more leisure business matters and social importance. The larger plantations many Southerners kept were filled with cotton, which was the main economical crop, although you could easily find rice fields scattered throughout the South. The larger plantation landowners normally possessed nearly twenty to fifty slaves.

The standard of living however for the slaves was much more disgraceful and discouraging, slaves were often kept in cramped quarters with little, if any, food, daily necessities, medicine, or clothing.

DEMOGRAPHICS

The American Confederation grew from thirteen to thirty six States, which allowed the U.S. to increase in territory, population, and wealth. The frontier territories became heavily populated in the last decade of the 18th, mainly with New Englanders. These frontier territories included Vermont, which became a state in 1791, Kentucky (1792), Tennessee (1796) and Ohio (1803).

The West was characterized by business prosperity until restrictions of business caused economic troubles to the East. Jefferson's Prohibition Trade Act and the War of 1812 were the main causes for those business and economic woes. A second wave of immigrants to place in 1806 resulted in the additions to the Union including Louisiana (1812), Indiana (1816), Mississippi (1817), Illinois (1818), and Alabama (1819).

Just prior to the Gold Rush slightly less than 19,000 individuals found their home near the Pacific Ocean; between the years of 1849 and 1860 more than 280,000 moved west and migrated near the Pacific Ocean.

 Growing Differences Between the North and South

The development of differences between the North and the South continued to grow, consisting of issues with slavery, taxes and the territories in the forum of the Congress of the United States. As long as neither side controlled the Senate, compromises were possible. Yet, tensions grew with both parties hoping to acquire new territories after the Louisiana Purchase and the Mexican War. Although the purchase of Alabama in 1819 provided a perfectly balanced Senate, the new territories were soon petitioned by both the North and South for the opportunity to acquire them.

Tensions mounted with the acquisition of the Kansas territory, John Brown's raid, the Dred Scott decision, and the split of the Democratic Party creating larger frustrations between the North and the South. The 1860 election seemed to be the final trigger for secession, and although many attempts for compromise were initiated, they ultimately failed. This set the stage for the Civil War.

SLAVERY AS A SOUTHERN INSTITUTION

The underlining concept of slavery was simple; slaves were considered property. The use of violence and cruelty forced slaves to never forget this particular concept. Although the image of slavery in the South was large plantations with hundreds of slaves and all citizens in the South kept slaves, the truth was only half of Southerners owned slaves and of those, eighty-eight percent owned twenty or fewer. The position of being a slave owner was thought to be only for the privileged and the rich.

Slaves were not only left to the planting and harvesting of the crops, slaves were also made to clear new land, dig ditches, care for and slaughter livestock, make repairs to buildings, and all other labor that came with running a farm or plantation. The grueling labor was always left to the male slaves, while the woman slaves tended to the house work of the plantation: cooking, cleaning, sewing and caring for the children. These slaves were often referred to as house servants, and while house servants benefited from work that was less strenuous then the field servants, they were under constant supervision of their owners.

Many South slave owners found that keeping a slave family together, the mother, father and children, gave them far greater advantages in respect to the economical outcome of crops, yet the majority of slave families were separated and sold off at the auction block.

The cotton gin was one of the most important inventions of the time. It was invented by Eli Whitney in 1793 and was used to separate the cotton from the seeds and seedpods. After this was invented the "industrialization of cotton" or the gin increased the financial benefit and importance of slavery greatly. From 1770-1800 the value of a slave had dropped by nearly fifty percent and the importance of having a slave began to dwindle. After the invention of the gin, the importance of slavery rose and the cost rose as well. A slave on the auction block after the invention of the cotton gin went from $50 to between the prices of $500 to $800.

IMPORTANCE OF COTTON

Before the 18th century, clothing was unsuitable and the garments worn were very difficult to keep clean. Cotton was the major product that could produce suitable garments, but it was also an expensive product. Cotton took time to produce. Before cotton industrialization, in the late 1700's; it took more than twelve to fourteen man-days to produce a pound of cotton. When Eli Whitney invented the cotton gin the cost of producing cotton became dramatically lower, which altered the production of cotton in the U.S., making it an economical exploitation for the South. Cotton industrialization was even more financially beneficial to the growth of the South.

On the Southern plantations a slave could now produce fifty pounds of raw cotton daily, this was huge compared to the previous amount of time it took a slave to only produce one pound. The process not only helped the Southern plantations produce the cotton faster, but also more cost effectively. The price of cotton a yard fell ninety percent; this caused the demand for cotton clothing to soar soon making it America's largest export.

In the early 1800s Britain, a major purchaser of cotton from the South used more than 79 million pounds of raw cotton, of which forty-eight percent came from the South. Just twenty years later imports were closer to 248 million, seventy percent came from the South and in 1860 over 1,000 million pounds were being used by Britain, while ninety-two percent of that cotton was coming from Southern plantations.

LIVING CONDITION OF SLAVES

Life was hard and work was tough for slaves working in America, quarters were small, crude, susceptible to weather, disease and often without basic necessities. Food was barely enough to keep them from starving, let alone maintain a healthy diet for the heavy workload they endured. Bedding and clothing was also very minimal.

Servant slaves fared far better off than the field servants, because they often were dressed to meet and greet guests and were normally given the hand-me-downs from the mistress of the house. They also had constant access to food in the kitchen and in food stores.

Slaves were often left without medication or care when they would get ill and were often still made to work in the hot and humid conditions of the South. Child mortality was extremely high on plantations, about sixty percent of slave children died. It was much higher for the rice plantations; they held a ninety percent child mortality rate. The constant threat of being sold was far worse for many of the slave families then the thought of acquiring an illness.

When slaves were thought to get out of hand owners would punish the slaves with horrific, hostile and brutal ways such as whipping, torturing, mutilation, imprisonment or being sold. Slaves were forbidden to ever strike an owner or any other white, for any reason even if it was in self-defense. And this was only one of the appalling rules laid out by Congress for slaves called the slave codes.

Although every state carried their own sets of codes and every states codes varied, the basic rules included, slaves were considered property and they were to be treated as just that, slaves could not testify in court against a white, they could not make contracts, buy or sell goods, own firearms, possess anti-slavery literature, gather without whites present, or visit the homes of whites or free blacks. The killing of a slave was almost never murder and the rape of a slave woman was treated as a form of trespassing.

ABOLITION MOVEMENT

The abolition movement began long before the time emancipation came about. The first great awakening began in the late 18th century, and the second in the early 19th century at the time of colonial settlements and mainly consisted of religious revivals and meetings. The meetings promoted the notion that all humans were free to renounce their sins and achieve salvation. They also posited that slavery was a byproduct of personal sin and they implied that emancipation was the price for repentance. This message came to the conclusion that a person should save their neighbors. Southern Kentucky was home to the first of such meetings with more than 10,000 participants.

In 1833 the American Anti-Slavery Society was founded and their (estimated) tens of thousands of members condemned slavery as a racial discriminating practice and as a moral sin. Many of these groups met opposition from slaveholders and rejections from national religious institutions. Opponents attempted to suppress the groups with enactments from churches and states and by using mob violence.

Many followed the lead of William Lloyd Garrison, who abandoned the churches believing they were corrupted by slavery. Garrison wanted to achieve a universal reform including the extension of women's rights, pacifism and temperance. The American Anti-Slavery Society committed to the political practices of Garrison and began to advocate for the dissolution of the Union with slave holding states. Garrison also used radical techniques to awaken Northerners by appointing a woman, Maria Weston

Chapman, as the overseer of the society's main office. Garrison also used women for traveling lecturers such as Sojourner Truth, Elizabeth Cady Stanton, Abby Kelley, Lucy Stone and dozens more women who all met with opposition and threats of physical harm.

Religious abolitionists formed the American and Foreign Anti-Slavery Society. This group continued to lobby religious institutions and gained valuable associates in the 1840's from the Methodist, Baptist and Presbyterian churches. Their resolve to gain anti-slavery support from religious institutions often caused the division of many local religious foundations.

These political and religious groups continued to focus their attention on the dismantling of slavery and made major gains until the Civil War, especially during the 1850's. Though they continued to grow in membership through the abolition movement, they still remained a minority and few free blacks in the Northern states received equal treatment.

LEADERS

Some abolition groups supported the abolition movement through churches and other organizations, while others used the political scene. Politically focused abolitionists lobbied legislatures and grilled political candidates on issues of slavery. The federal government's resistance to the lobbying and petitioning of these groups forced political abolitionists to form their own party to pursue emancipation in 1840 called the Liberty Party.

Several of the abolition leaders came from New England including William Allen, the founding member and director of the African Institution who assisted for many years as a committee member of the Society for the Abolition of the Slave Trade. Henry Ward Beecher was another, the brother to Harriett Beecher Stowe who authored the famous book *Uncle Tom's Cabin* and was supporter of emancipation. John Brown was the first white American to advocate and practice insurrection as a means to the abolition of slavery. Wendell Phillips, a graduate from Harvard Law School, stopped practicing law in 1836 to dedicate himself to the abolitionist cause of William Lloyd Garrison. Theodore Dwight Weld was one of the leading founders of the American abolition movement and played a key role as a writer, editor and speaker. He is best known for his work *American Slavery as It Is: Testimony of a Thousand Witnesses*. Arthur Tappan was the co-founder of the American Anti-Slavery Society and served as its first President until he resigned when the group began to support woman suffrage and feminism. He and his brother then founded the American and Foreign Anti-Slavery Society. Robert Purvis, member of a prominent family in South Carolina, helped establish the American Anti-Slavery Society and the Library Company of Colored People. He was a large supporter of the Underground Railroad and is estimated to have helped one slave escape to freedom a day. By that account he would have helped 9,000 people find freedom.

These were only a few of the major leaders in the resolution of slavery. Other prominent leaders in the fight for emancipation from the start of the country included; John Quincy Adams, John Jay, Alexander Hamilton, Aaron Burr, Sojourner Truth, Elizabeth Cady Stanton, John Rankin, Henry Stanton, James Sherman, John Parker, and many others.

METHODS AND TACTICS OF ABOLITION

One of the first methods of abolitionists was to spread the word and gather like-minded individuals together. It was when this method began that the formations of many abolition groups were formed. One such group was the American Anti-Slavery Society who focused on putting together lectures in an attempt to show the moral and religious consequences of slavery, hoping to change the minds and hearts of non-slaveholders. Many abolition groups found these tactics to be inadequate and they turned their attention to more political methods.

Another method abolitions used to get their message out was through published literature. This tactic included the publication of pamphlets and leaflets that included sermons, songs, essays, poetry and slogans that included an anti-slavery message. They also attempted to show the cruelty and animalist means of slavery through children's literature, attempting to awaken a younger audience and following, although this sort of literature was outlawed in the Southern states.

Newspapers were also important to abolitionists to get their message across. *The Liberator*, published by William Lloyd Garrison, was one of many newspapers that attacked the immoral sanction of slavery.

One of the most famous activities and tactics of the abolition movement was the Underground Railroad where slaves were given the means to escape from slavery as well as the shelter, safety and guidance to be free. The Underground Railroad stretched from the Southern states all the way to Canada and was the first method where slaves could find solitude and safety from their slaveholders.

UNCLE TOM'S CABIN

The novel *Uncle Tom's Cabin* by Harriet Beecher Stowe, was about the evils of slavery and was influential in creating sentimental feelings against the institution of slavery. The tale centered on Uncle Tom, a long suffering black slave and the other slaves and owners that revolved around his life. It depicted the cruel realities of slavery as it showed the Christian values that love and faith can overcome anything evil, even slavery.

The novel was the best-selling novel of the 19th century and has been said to be a main source of the abolition movement. 300,000 copies of the book were sold the first year it was published in 1852. Its impact was so strong it was said to have laid the groundwork for the American Civil War – so much so that when the writer met with Abraham Lincoln he was said to have commented, "So, this is the little lady who made this big war."

RECONSTRUCTION ACTS

Two years after the Civil War the United Stated Congress passed four statutes, known as the Reconstruction Acts. The first was passed on March 2nd, 1867 to provide the more efficient Government of the Rebel states including Virginia, Texas, Florida, South Carolina, North Carolina, Mississippi, Alabama, Arkansas, Georgia, and Louisiana. The second, third, and fourth were passed to supplement the first act and to facilitate Restoration.

New constitutions were written in the South under the terms of the Reconstruction Acts. By 1868 Arkansas, North Carolina, South Carolina, Louisiana, Alabama and Florida were readmitted to the Union, after ratifying the 14th amendment required by the Reconstruction Act. Virginia, Mississippi, Texas and Georgia were readmitted in 1870.

FOURTEENTH AND FIFTEENTH AMENDMENTS

Three new constitutional amendments were adopted upon the end of the Civil War, the thirteenth abolished slavery and the fourteenth and fifteenth focused on the civil rights of slaves.

The fourteenth amendment to the United States constitution includes the Due Process and Equal Protection clauses among others. The fourteenth amendment requires that states provide protection under the law to all persons, granting all natural born or naturalized citizens federal and civil rights. The fourteenth amendment was exemplified during it interpretation to prohibit segregation in public schools and other facilities in Brown vs. Board of Education.

The fifteenth amendment states that the governments of the United States of America may not prevent a person from voting because of their race, color, or previous condition of servitude.

SCALAWAGS AND CARPETBAGGERS

Carpetbaggers were Northerners who moved to the South with freedmen. The phrase was originally coined from the term carpet bags, which are inexpensive luggage. A scalawag is a person who was White from the South who joined the Republican Party in the ex-Confederate area during reconstruction. Two of the most prominent Scalawags were General James Longstreet and Joseph Brown.

 The Spanish-American War

TELLER AMENDMENT

The Teller Amendment was passed just five days before the official start of the Spanish-American War. It stated that the United States had no intention to annex the island of Cuba, but was rather engaging in the Spanish-American War in order to liberate the Cuban people from Spanish rule in order to give them their independence. Passing this amendment reassured many that the war was not simply another imperialist quest for the United States – from a political viewpoint, the amendment was largely an attempt to minimize opposition to the war.

However, the amendment was used as justification after the war was ended for the United States to remain in Cuba for several years to ensure "pacification" continued, and later led to the Platt Amendment. This amendment allowed the U.S. government to overrule important decisions made by the Cuban government if they were not in the best interest of the United States. The Teller Amendment also led to the construction of a U.S. Naval Base in Guantanamo Bay.

FILIPINO INSURRECTION

As the Spanish-American War came to a close in August of 1898, Spain ceded the Islands of the Philippines to the United States. However, for over a decade Spain itself had been engaged in a heated war over Philippine independence, and the people of the Philippines had no intention of simply becoming subject to another world power. Despite the hopes of the Filipino people that the United States would soon leave their islands and grant them independence, American President William McKinley was fiercely determined to keep the country and colonize it.

The conflict, which came to be known as the Filipino Insurrection or Philippine-American War, waged on for three years, resulting in the death of over 4,000 American troops and over 500,000 Filipino citizens. Although the Filipino people surrendered in 1902, they continued to seek their independence, and were eventually established as the Commonwealth of the Philippines in 1935.

World War I – 1914-1929

The root cause for World War I was the assassination of the Archduke Francis Ferdinand on June 28, 1914. The so called Central Powers – Austria, Hungary, Germany, Turkey and Bulgaria – waged war against the Allied Nations, twenty-three in all, led by France and supported by Great Britain, the British Empire and Russia. The U.S. President at that time was Woodrow Wilson, who wanted the U.S. to be aloof. He wanted the U.S. to be "neutral in both thought and deed."

The trade and commerce between U.S. on the one side and Britain and France on the other, was at a roaring high and this had created a soft corner for the Allies in the U.S.

During the War, Germans became a target of hate with their use of submarines against soft, commercial targets. In the year 1915, the British ship "Lusitania" was torpedoed mercilessly and sunk by the German submarines; approximately 125 American lives were lost. Wilson raised a very strong protest and Germany assured that it would not target neutral nations. In 1917, Germany went back on its word and attacked both Allies and neutrals through its awesome submarine power.

On April 6, 1917, the U.S. declared war against Germany. Millions of men in the army were dispatched to Europe. The AEF – American Expeditionary Force – under General John J. Pershing, in France, started winning battle after battle, which resulted in Germany asking for an Armistice on November 11, 1918.

As a result of the war, many industries began to flourish. Shipbuilding, airplane manufacture, tanks and other artillery manufacture, were thriving. Innovation and sophistication were achieved in many production units. Those manufacturing units that were engaged in the manufacture of uniforms for soldiers were converted into garment-making factories. Because of the war, there was prosperity in the U.S.

The building industry witnessed a boom. Many skyscrapers including the Empire State building in New York were built. Railroads, highways, waterways and other infrastructure was built. The automobile industry thrived. There was general prosperity all around, and the lifestyle of common people changed as the standard of living improved beyond compare.

World War II – 1939-1945

In the 1930s, the Axis countries of Germany, Italy and Japan started swallowing smaller nations in Europe, one by one – Albania, Austria, Czechoslovakia as well as Ethiopia.

In Asia, Japan seized Manchuria and attacked China. These happenings from 1937 to 1939 were a prelude to World War II. The U.S. felt that if the whole of Europe and Asia were conquered by the Axis powers, then the New World would also face imminent danger of attack.

The U.S. wisely began to strengthen its military might and then advised all the nations in South and North America to rally round as one nation in order to defend the continent from fascist forces if they were to strike. Hitler's Germany dragged Europe into war in late 1939.

President Roosevelt dispatched fifty destroyers to England to enable them to fight the Axis effectively. In exchange, the U.S. was allowed to have air and naval bases on smaller Atlantic islands ranging from British Guiana to Newfoundland. Germans decimated many towns and cities in Europe with their well-organized air power. The other Axis powers, Italy and Japan, brought in destruction in other parts of Europe and Asia respectively.

The U.S. policy of "isolationism" had to change because of mounting public opinion. On August 14, 1941, "The Atlantic Charter" was signed by both President Roosevelt of the U.S. and Prime Minister Winston Churchill of the U.K. It was welcomed by the public as it envisioned a general security system for a warless world, which would remain in effect for a long time.

Then without any provocation from the U.S. side, the Japanese attacked the U.S. Naval base in Pearl Harbor, Hawaii. As per their formal agreement, the other Axis powers joined together and declared war against the U.S. The Pearl Harbor attack was followed by the Japanese capturing the Philippine Islands, Guam and Wake Island from the U.S.

When pushed into war, the U.S. could not keep quiet. The nation led the Allies to resounding victories in the Soviet Union, Egypt and the Pacific. The U.S. Supreme commander, General Dwight Eisenhower, led the allied forces to victory, battle after battle in Europe. The Allies landed on the shores of Normandy, France on June 6, 1944, which was called "D Day".

German forces were rendered ineffective and the Allies achieved peace on May 8, 1945, a day which became known as Victory in Europe Day – V.E. Day. The Philippine

Islands were wrested back from Japan and the battles of Okinawa and Iwo Jima were won.

The first nuclear bomb was hurled at Hiroshima of Japan, killing hundreds of thousands of people. This was too great a shock for the Japanese and the Emperor of Japan intervened to stop further onslaught and mayhem. On September 2, 1945, Japan signed a formal peace agreement and the war ended. With this victory, the United States of America had become a global super power.

ROSIE RIVETER

At the beginning of World War II, it became necessary for women to work and hold the jobs that men had left vacant. However, the government was not satisfied with women's response to the call to work. Rosie the Riveter was part of a propaganda campaign to sell the importance of the war effort and lure women into working. A fictional character, Rosie the Riveter was portrayed as the ideal woman worker: loyal, efficient, patriotic, and pretty. A song titled "Rosie the Riveter" became popular in 1942. Norman Rockwell's image on the cover of the Saturday Evening Post was the first widely publicized pictorial representation of Rosie. This led to many other Rosie images and women to represent that image. The most famous image of Rosie appeared in the government-commissioned "We Can Do It" poster.

At the start of World War II, everyone had agreed that women workers were greatly needed, but only as a temporary arrangement. After the war, the cultural division of labor by sex reasserted itself. Many women remained in the workforce but employers forced them back into lower-paying female jobs. Most women were laid off and told to go back to their homes.

DOUBLE "V" CAMPAIGN

In 1942, a letter was sent to the Pittsburgh Courier. A man by the name of James G. Thompson was calling for a "Double V" or "double victory" campaign to take place. This campaign's goal was to reach two major victories. The first was victory over Axis powers that were present in World War II, the second was power over racism in the United States. Thompson was concerned with discrimination in the war and in general. He proposed that providing equal rights for African Americans wasn't such a high price to pay when they were sacrificing their lives in the war. American troops were segregated throughout the war. The Double Victory Campaign raised was another small step towards complete emancipation.

The Cold War

The Soviet Union and its East European allies, all of whom embraced communism, occupied more than fifty percent of Europe. The Soviets' hold in Asia was also sizable. Totalitarianism under the garb of Communism threatened democracies and capitalistic free market economies all over the world. Though the U.S., the U.K. and Canada were the only countries known to possess a nuclear arsenal, the Soviets also had an atomic energy stockpile.

This resulted in an arms race, feeding into the U.S. developing ICBMs and other missiles capable of mass destruction. The U.S. and the Soviets also entered into a satellite race. There was mutual suspicion and distrust among them. The Soviets also wanted to stockpile nuclear missiles in Cuba. Had Soviets succeeded, those in the U.S. would have had to live in perpetual fear. This is commonly referred to as the Cuban Missile Crisis.

President John F. Kennedy stood firm and averted what would have been the most destructive war ever seen. In 1947 peace treaties were signed with Italy, Romania, Hungary and Bulgaria. However, the Soviets thwarted all efforts to make treaties with Austria and Germany. As a result Germany was divided – East under Soviet Russia and the West under the Allies. Ultimately, with the collapse of the U.S.S.R., the Germans again had a unified Germany.

DR. STRANGELOVE

How I Learned to Stop Worrying and Love the Bomb, or, as it was more commonly known - *Dr. Strangelove*, was a movie released at the height of the Cold War in 1964. *Dr. Strangelove* is a political satire centered on the question of nuclear war. The movie was released not long after the Cuban Missile Crisis and launch of Sputnik. It was a time of widespread worry about the possibility of nuclear war. The film depicts the events and decisions by government officials leading to such a war in a comical way. The film came as a great shock to most audiences, and despite the government's best efforts, created a feeling of mistrust in many minds. Today *Dr. Strangelove* continues to be an example of Cold War ideology.

ALGER HISS

Alger Hiss was born in Baltimore and attended Johns Hopkins University and Harvard Law School. He served as a law clerk to a Supreme Court Justice, went on to work in the Roosevelt administration, then served as Secretary General. Hiss was present during the formative years of the United Nations.

In 1939, former member of the U.S. Communist Party Whitaker Chambers told Assistant Secretary of State Adolf Berle that Hiss was a communist. Though accused multiple times throughout his life of spying for the Soviet Union, he was never convicted for espionage. He was however accused in a perjury trial of lying about having passed State Department papers to Chambers and was sentenced to two years in prison. He vehemently denied the charges for the duration of his life.

HUNGARIAN UPRISING

After Stalin's death 1953 the world looked to see what changes would be made to the political scene of Eastern Europe. This included the country of Hungary which was increasingly less satisfied with their situation under communist rule, and was arguing for democratic rule. In response, Communist Party officials placed Imre Nagy, known for his opposition to Stalin's policies, as the new premier. At Nagy's request the Soviets even withdrew their troops. However, as Nagy took further anti-Communist actions such as abandoning the one-party system and attempting to withdraw from the Soviet bloc, they returned in force. In November of 1956, Soviet tanks invaded Budapest and killed nearly 3,000 citizens. Over 200,000 more were forced to flee the country. Although the United States publicly stated their support of the Hungarian people's cause, nothing was ever done to help the Hungarian people.

 The Korean and Vietnam War

To fight communism, the U.S., no longer a recluse, had to support South Korea against communist North Korea. Likewise, to combat the spread of communism in South East Asia, it had to fight in Vietnam. Then, in order to combat terrorism, the U.S. had to wage a war in Afghanistan, which had not only encouraged terrorism but also given a free rein to Al Qaeda, a most destructive terrorist group and its leader Osama Bin Laden, who was largely believed to have masterminded the infamous 9/11 attacks inside the U.S. Again the U.S. had to wage a war on Iraq to end the rule of a loathsome dictator and establish democracy.

GULF OF TONKIN RESOLUTION

Early in 1964, military activity in Vietnam was still relatively centralized and small. Although plans had been made to expand tactics more aggressively, action had not been taken. In August, there were reports of U.S. destroyers stationed in the Gulf of Tonkin (in Vietnam) being attacked by North Vietnam forces. President Johnson took immediate action and proposed the Gulf of Tonkin Resolution which would give him power to expand military efforts in Vietnam in any way that he deemed necessary to establish peace in the area.

The Resolution quickly passed and President Johnson was able to retaliate. However, it later became known that the claimed attack in the Gulf of Tonkin had not actually occurred and many felt that Congress had been deceived into supporting the Resolution. It was repealed six years later.

The Results of War

- The war between the colonists and the British Empire was fought to gain independence.
- The Mexican War resulted in more land being included in the U.S.
- The Civil War saw the establishment of the telegraph throughout. More areas came into the United States possession. A long lasting democracy took root.
- The Spanish War established an otherwise aloof United States as a world power.
- World War I saw a "neutral in thought and deed" America sucked into war. The U.S. had become the supplier of most sophisticated war weapons including warships, warplanes and submarines, tanks, etc. After the war, there was all-round development. Infrastructure, highways, waterways, and railroads developed at a breathtaking speed. Both agriculture and industries thrived.
- World War II established the U.S. as one of the super powers. It also saw the use of the nuclear bomb. The U.S. almost spent one hundred billion dollars to build its war efforts. The economy boomed after the war and there was a tremendous boost to employment.
- In 1977, President Jimmy Carter held Peace Talks at Camp David between Egyptian President Anwar Sadat and Israeli Prime Minister Menachem Begin. This was a monumental achievement in negotiations that began the framework for peace in the Middle East. In his speech to congress, Carter said "Blessed are the peacemakers, for they shall be the children of God."

The Development of American Political Parties

During President George Washington's tenure there were two factions, the Federalists, who supported the constitution and the Non-Federalists, or, the Democratic-Republicans, who opposed it. Federalists were led by the Secretary of the Treasury Alexander Hamilton duly supported by George Washington himself. The Federalists were men of letters and means and were occupying high social positions.

The second faction was led by Thomas Jefferson and James Madison and called themselves as "Democratic-Republicans." Their constituency was made up of Southern and Mid-Atlantic States, comprising mainly of small property owners, small farmers, and local political leaders. They started to dominate the political scene. By the 1820's, the Federalists lost steam and were defunct.

When Andrew Jackson became President in the year 1828, the "Democratic-Republican Party" launched by Jefferson and Madison renamed itself the "Democratic party." It became a party with a mass following and has remained dominant ever since.

Between 1828 and 1856 the Democratic Party faced severe opposition from a party known as the "Whig Party." The Whig Party had a following mainly in the New England area and from the business class. Though democrats ruled the roost, the Whigs also had their hour of glory – they had two presidents in William Henry Harrison (he died after only one month in office and John Tyler, his deputy, became president) and Zachary Taylor. The Whig-Democrats rivalry extended to state and local levels. By the 1850's, the Whig party faded into insignificance and became defunct.

In the year 1854, Franklin Pierce, then Democratic President, brought in the inflammatory Kansas-Nebraska Act. This was the prime reason for establishing an Anti-Slavery Party, better known as the "Republican Party." Most members of the "Whig Party" joined the Republican Party. When the Republican candidate Abraham Lincoln became President in 1860, the Republicans, though mainly formed to resist slavery, increased their following by including northern industrialists, merchants, workers, farmers as well as those slaves who were set free. On the other hand, the "Democratic Party" broke into Northern and Southern factions. The Democrats survived the civil war, but could not gain the Presidency for nearly fifty years, with the exception of 1882-1892.

As Ronald Reagan was approaching his run for a second term as president in 1984, his concern was less with solidifying the Republican voters in his own party, and more with swaying liberal and Democratic voters to support him. One way that he did this was by mentioning a new Bruce Springsteen song, Born in the USA, in a campaign speech. Ironically, Bruce Springsteen was an ardent liberal and the song was a criticism of the Vietnam War and treatment of veterans, but this didn't matter in the end. It has now become famous as a patriotic song, and used in many more presidential campaigns through the years.

The two-party system – Republicans and Democrats – has been evolving for quite some time and today has reached sophistication and maturity.

OTHER POLITICAL PARTIES

- The "Anti-Masons," a third party, emerged during the 1820's. They challenged privileges under the Masonic symbol.
- In the year 1840, the "Liberty Party" came into being; they predominantly identified themselves as the anti-slavery political party.
- In the 1850's, "The American Party" (a.k.a. "Know-Nothing-Party") got good backing. They fought for limiting immigration, specifically, the immigration of Irish-Catholics.
- In the 1870's, the "Greenback Party" was launched mainly to bring in paper currency. They rejected the gold standard.
- In the 1880's the "Populist Party" (a.k.a. "the people's party") came into being in the areas where farming was done such as the Midwest, South and Far West. Government control of railroads, direct election of U.S. senators, graduated income tax, minting coins in silver and not gold, were some of their demands. They had a socialistic outlook.
- In the early 1900's, the "Socialist Party" launched by Eugene Debs was prominent.
- The "Bull Moose Party," the "Progressive Party," and "the American Independent Party" also briefly appeared in the political scene.

All the third parties as well as independent candidates contributed usefully towards the maturity of a sophisticated party system that was unique to the United States.

There were local parties and state parties as well. However, since media campaigns have become structural to suit the personality of the candidates, local and state parties have lost what normally used to be their traditional roles. The local and state parties, under the changing scenario, confine themselves to fund-raising as well as offering specialized professional services to prospective candidates.

The American political system has always opted for a two party system against a multi-party system. Thomas Reed, speaker of the house, in 1880, said: "…The best system is to have one party to govern and the other party watch…" Over the years, the two party system has acquired a high degree of maturity and third parties have always found it tough to elect their candidates for the congress or state legislatures. Americans rely on the "single member district" principle wherein whichever candidate gets the most votes in a legislative district represents that district. In such a scenario, there won't be any scope for a third party to garner votes.

The election of the chief executive is also unique. In most democracies, the leader of the house is chosen by the elected parliamentarians on the floor of the house. In contrast, the President of the United States is chosen by a separate election process. Two parties following middle of the road policies contest and the one which presents its case most effectively is chosen.

Welfare Programs

THE NEW DEAL

The New Deal reforms were at the root of all welfare legislation in the United States. The most prominent among New Deal legislation was the Social Security Act of 1935 which aimed at unemployment compensation, aid to dependent children, old age assistance, and aid to States for Pensions as well as grants to States for maternal services.

When Lyndon Johnson was the President, very laudable welfare legislations under the heading "Great Society" were attempted in 1960's. In 1965, Congress passed legislation devised to:

- Provide medical aid to the old, disabled and indigent through Medicare and Medicaid.
- Provide aid to public schools and educational loans to college students to further their studies.
- To aid poor people by supplementing their rents.
- To institute loans, grants and training programs for health care professionals so as to make them effective.
- Development assistance to be provided to Appalachia. John F. Kennedy, during his election campaign, found the people of "Appalachia" – a region representing Mississippi to New York State along the Appalachian Mountains – lived in penury and inhuman conditions.

SOCIAL INSURANCE

- **Social Security (a.k.a. OASDI – Old Age, Survivors, Disability Insurance)**
It is the country's major cash transfer program. It pays approximately 52 million persons over sixty-five years of age. This program is financed by payroll taxes split in equal proportions between employee and employer. Government employees are not eligible for OASDI who are otherwise covered by an adequate federal pension plan. A large proportion of all non-governmental payrolls are covered by OASDI. A prorated share of an employee's wages is received for social security and the payments to the affected are also prorated based on the basis of their previous job incomes. Inflation-related adjustments are taken into account while paying benefits.

- **Federal-State Unemployment Compensation**
The labor department of the federal government administers this program with the help of different state employment agencies. It is a state-funded project. A tax on employers – between 0.5 to 4.8 percent of total wages paid – is levied. The rate varies between states. Also, the eligibility criteria, the outer time limit for giving

benefits and benefits itself, differ from state to state. However, it is seen that most states provide basic coverage for twenty-six weeks. A federal legislation during 1980's extended the coverage for an additional thirteen to twenty-six weeks. The coverage is meant for workers who were seen to have had a history of regular employment and lost their jobs. A domestic worker is not covered. Also those who held no regular jobs were also excluded.

MEDICARE

Established in the year 1965, Medicare is one of the programs that have become the mainstay of welfare state programs. Medicare imparts assistance in the form of payments to (1) all citizens eligible for social security, (2) disabled persons and, (3) any citizen with kidney failure.

PUBLIC ASSISTANCE

There are mainly five principle public assistance programs:
1. Medicaid
2. SSI
3. AFDC
4. Food Stamps
5. Public Housing
6. Other Programs

1. Medicaid is a state-option program, designed to help persons in need of medical assistance. Every state has its own eligibility and disbursement rules. Medicaid has, over the years, become the largest federal "in-kind" assistance program.

2. SSI (Supplemental Security Income) came into being in 1974. It is aimed at imparting additional help to aged, disabled, and blind citizens. This program pays benefits on the criteria of need. It is entirely financed by the federal government.

3. AFDC (Aid to Families with Dependent Children) is planned so that the benefits of this program are meant only for families with a dependent child. Each state has its own rules for benefits. You may note that this and SSI are the two programs that pay cash to recipients.

4. Food Stamps is designed for those who receive public assistance as well as those citizens whose income is less than a stated standard, who are provided with food stamps (coupons) and/or money for food. It is a federal and state jointly administered program. The program, however, is totally financed by the federal government. This program has been criticized severely by congressmen from 1983 onwards because of its open-ended nature.

5. <u>Public Housing</u> provides a comfortable, low-cost living space in a congenial environment for the poor and needy citizens of the society. The intent is laudable but administration has not been above reproach. Construction delays, scandal, and administrative hurdles have all been faced. In 1970's the Department of Housing and Urban Development devised a housing grant instead of a building a house on public financing, but this form of aid had lost the favor of the Reagan administration. Housing allowances, rent subsidies, interest supplements – all these and more were tried with no conspicuous success.

6. <u>Other Programs</u> WIC (Women, Infants and Children), a program aimed at alleviating the problems of the poor and downtrodden, was in fact a nutritional supplement program funded by the federal government. Some other programs like breakfast and lunch programs for school children, preschool programs for poor children, medical programs and vocational guidance programs have also been tried.

With any governmental program, though the intent is good and the content exceptional, the execution lacks in direction, speed and sincerity of purpose.

Constitutional Amendments

There have been twenty-seven constitutional amendments made in total to the Constitution of the United States of America so far. The original ten amendments, which are better known as the Bill of Rights, were ratified on December 15, 1791 and were followed by other important amendments that have not stopped touching the lives of the common man. Additionally, there have been amendments which deal in governance, administration and powers of elected legislators.

Amendment I
Congress shall make no law respecting an establishment of religion, or prohibiting the free exercise thereof; or abridging the freedom of speech, or of the press; or the right of the people peaceably to assemble, and to petition the Government for a redress of grievances.

Amendment II
A well-regulated Militia, being necessary to the security of a free State, the right of the people to keep and bear Arms, shall not be infringed.

Amendment III
No soldier shall, in time of peace be quartered in any house, without the consent of the Owner, nor in time of war, but in a manner to be prescribed by law.

Amendment IV

The right of the people to be secure in their persons, houses, papers, and effects, against unreasonable searches and seizures, shall not be violated, and no Warrants shall issue, but upon probable cause, supported by Oath or affirmation, and particularly describing the place to be searched, and the persons or things to be seized.

Amendment V

No person shall be held to answer for a capital, or otherwise infamous crime, unless on a presentment or indictment of a Grand Jury, except in cases arising in the land or naval forces, or in the Militia, when in actual service in time of War or public danger; nor shall any person be subject for the same offence to be twice put in jeopardy of life or limb; nor shall be compelled in any criminal case to be a witness against himself, nor be deprived of life, liberty, or property, without due process of law; nor shall private property be taken for public use, without just compensation.

Amendment VI

In all criminal prosecutions, the accused shall enjoy the right to a speedy and public trial, by an impartial jury of the State and district wherein the crime shall have been committed, which district shall have been previously ascertained by law, and to be informed of the nature and cause of the accusation; to be confronted with the witnesses against him; to have compulsory process for obtaining witnesses in his favor, and to have the Assistance of Counsel for his defense.

Amendment VII

In Suits at common law, where the value in controversy shall exceed twenty dollars, the right of trial by jury shall be preserved, and no fact tried by a jury, shall be otherwise re-examined in any Court of the United States, than according to the rules of the common law.

Amendment VIII

Excessive bail shall not be required, nor excessive fines imposed, nor cruel and unusual punishments inflicted.

Amendment IX

The enumeration in the Constitution, of certain rights, shall not be construed to deny or disparage others retained by the people.

Amendment X

The powers not delegated to the United States by the Constitution, nor prohibited by it to the States, are reserved to the States respectively, or to the people.

Amendment XIII
Section 1. Neither slavery nor involuntary servitude, except as a punishment for crime whereof the party shall have been duly convicted, shall exist within the United States, or any place subject to their jurisdiction.

Section 2. Congress shall have power to enforce this article by appropriate legislation.

Amendment XIV
Section 1. All persons born or naturalized in the United States, and subject to the jurisdiction thereof, are citizens of the United States and of the State wherein they reside. No State shall make or enforce any law which shall abridge the privileges or immunities of citizens of the United States; nor shall any State deprive any person of life, liberty, or property, without due process of law; nor deny to any person within its jurisdiction the equal protection of the laws.

Section 2. Representatives shall be apportioned among the several States according to their respective numbers, counting the whole number of persons in each State, excluding Indians not taxed. But when the right to vote at any election for the choice of electors for President and Vice President of the United States, Representatives in Congress, the Executive and Judicial officers of a State, or the members of the Legislature thereof, is denied to any of the male inhabitants of such State, being twenty-one years of age, and citizens of the United States, or in any way abridged, except for participation in rebellion, or other crime, the basis of representation therein shall be reduced in the proportion which the number of such male citizens shall bear to the whole number of male citizens twenty-one years of age in such State.

Section 3. No person shall be a Senator or Representative in Congress, or elector of President and Vice President, or hold any office, civil or military, under the United States, or under any State, who, having previously taken an oath, as a member of Congress, or as an officer of the United States, or as a member of any State legislature, or as an executive or judicial officer of any State, to support the Constitution of the United States, shall have engaged in insurrection or rebellion against the same, or given aid or comfort to the enemies thereof. But Congress may by a vote of two-thirds of each House, remove such disability.

Section 4. The validity of the public debt of the United States, authorized by law, including debts incurred for payment of pensions and bounties for services in suppressing insurrection or rebellion, shall not be questioned. But neither the United States nor any State shall assume or pay any debt or obligation incurred in aid of insurrection or rebellion against the United States, or any claim for the loss or emancipation of any slave; but all such debts, obligations and claims shall be held illegal and void.

Section 5. The Congress shall have power to enforce, by appropriate legislation, the provisions of this article.

Amendment XV
Section 1. The right of citizens of the United States to vote shall not be denied or abridged by the United States or by any State on account of race, color, or previous condition of servitude.

Section 2. The Congress shall have power to enforce this article by appropriate legislation.

Amendment XIX
The right of citizens of the United States to vote shall not be denied or abridged by the United States or by any State on account of sex.

Congress shall have power to enforce this article by appropriate legislation.

Amendment XXIV
Section 1. The right of citizens of the United States to vote in any primary or other election for President or Vice President, for electors for President or Vice President, or for Senator or Representative in Congress, shall not be denied or abridged by the United States or any state by reason of failure to pay any poll tax or other tax.

Section 2. The Congress shall have power to enforce this article by appropriate legislation.

Amendment XXVI
Section 1. The right of citizens of the United States, who are 18 years of age or older, to vote, shall not be denied or abridged by the United States or any state on account of age.

Section 2. The Congress shall have the power to enforce this article by appropriate legislation.

The Supreme Court

The Supreme Court is the highest court in the country. It's made up of eight justices and one Chief Justice. Justices are appointed to their positions by the President with the approval of the Senate. Because justices, like other federal judges, serve until death, retirement, or impeachment, these appointments are extremely important.

While the Supreme Court is asked to revisit an average of 7,500 cases every year, they generally review less than one hundred of them. The cases heard by the Supreme Court and their decisions regarding those cases can have long-term effects for society. For example, the Supreme Court's 1954 decision to desegregate schools in Brown v. Board of Education of Topeka led to the eventual desegregation of schools all across the United States. Despite the Court's important ruling, however, some school systems remained segregated up until 1970. The Executive and Legislative branches would have been responsible for ensuring the schools took the appropriate steps following the decision, since the Court can only interpret the law, not enforce it.

Twice a week, the justices convene to go over cases that could possibly be reviewed. For a case to be selected for review, four of the justices must agree to hear it. If a case is not selected, then the decision handed down by the lower courts is deemed to be final.

After hearing a case, the Supreme Court justices have a conference to determine their decisions. Each justice writes down his or her decision about the case and the vote is recorded. Only five votes are needed to finalize a decision.

Once the decision is reached, it is written out by the justices along with the reasons used for reaching that decision. Justices who do not agree with the majority can write a dissenting opinion which is recorded.

As explained above, the Supreme Court is important because its decisions have widespread effects not just for the individuals involved in the cases it reviews but every citizen of the United States. Because the law is not clearly spelled out, the justices have to determine how laws apply to different situations, as well as what the authors of the Constitution intended for some of the passages to mean.

The Legislature, the Executive and the Judiciary form the backbone of the U.S. administrative system. Of the three, the judiciary with the Supreme Court at the apex has exceptional powers to correct an erring legislature or the executive.

Summary of Supreme Court Jurisdiction

Original Jurisdiction	Appellate Jurisdiction*
A. Mandatory (must be heard by court) 1. Disputes between states	1. Cases in which a federal court has held an act of Congress unconstitutional, if the federal government is a party, any cases in which a state supreme court has held an act of Congress to be unconstitutional 2. Cases in which a state court has upheld a state law against a claim that it conflicts with the constitution or federal law 3. Cases in which a federal court has overturned a state law on the grounds that it conflicts with the constitution or federal law 4. Decisions of special three-judge federal district courts
B. Discretionary (Court need not hear) 1. Cases brought by a state 2. Disputes between a state and the federal government 3. Cases involving foreign diplomatic personnel	1. All decisions of federal courts of appeals except those in mandatory categories 2. All decisions of the highest state courts involving issues of federal law, except those in mandatory categories

Important Supreme Court Cases

In the case of the Bill of Rights, the Supreme Court under Chief Justice John Marshall ruled in the case Barron v. Baltimore, (1833) that the Bill of Rights applied only to the Federal Government and is not binding on the states.

1803 – Marbury v. Madison – Often called the most important decision in the history of the Supreme Court, Marbury v. Madison established the principle of judicial review and the power of the Court to determine the constitutionality of legislative and executive acts.

The case arose from a political dispute in the aftermath of the presidential election of 1800 in which Thomas Jefferson, a Democratic-Republican, defeated the incumbent president, John Adams, a Federalist. In the closing days of Adams's administration, the Federalist-dominated Congress created a number of judicial positions, including forty-two Justices of the Peace for the District of Columbia. The Senate confirmed the appointments, the President signed them, and it was the responsibility of the Secretary of State to seal the commissions and deliver them. In the rush of last-minute activities, the outgoing Secretary of State failed to deliver commissions to four justices of the peace, including William Marbury.

The new Secretary of State under President Jefferson, James Madison, refused to deliver the commissions because the new administration was angry that the Federalists had tried to entrench members of their party in the judiciary. Marbury brought suit in the Supreme Court to order Madison to deliver his commission.

If the Court sided with Marbury, Madison might still have refused to deliver the commission, and the Court had no way to enforce the order. If the Court ruled against Marbury, it risked surrendering judicial power to the Jeffersonians by allowing them to deny Marbury the office he was legally entitled to. Chief Justice John Marshall resolved this dilemma by ruling that the Supreme Court did not have authority to act in this case. Marshall stated that Section 13 of the Judiciary Act, which gave the Court that power, was unconstitutional because it enlarged the Court's original jurisdiction from the jurisdiction defined by the Constitution itself. By deciding not to decide in this case, the Supreme Court secured its position as the final arbiter of the law.

1824 – Gibbons B. Ogden – The first government of the United States under the Articles of Confederation was weak, partly because it lacked the power to regulate the new nation's economy, including the flow of interstate commerce. The Constitution gave the U.S. Congress the power "to regulate commerce...among the several states....," but that authority was challenged frequently by states that wanted to retain control over economic matters.

In the early 1800s, the state of New York passed a law that required steamboat operators who traveled between New York and New Jersey to obtain a license from New York. Aaron Ogden possessed such a license; Thomas Gibbons did not. When Ogden learned that Gibbons was competing with him, and without permission from New York, Ogden sued to stop Gibbons.

Gibbons held a federal license to navigate coastal waters under the Coasting Act of 1793, but the New York State courts agreed with Ogden that Gibbons had violated the law because he did not have a New York State license. When Gibbons took his case to the Supreme Court, however, the justices struck down the New York law as unconstitutional because it infringed on the U.S. Congress's power to regulate commerce. "The word 'to regulate' implies, in its nature, full power over the thing to be regulated," the Court said. Therefore, "it excludes, necessarily, the action of all others that would perform the same operation on the same thing."

1856 – Dred Scott v. Sanford – Dred Scott was a slave whose owner, John Emerson, took him from Missouri, a state that allowed slavery, to Illinois, where slavery was prohibited. Several years later Scott returned to Missouri with Emerson. Scott believed that because he had lived in a free state, he should no longer be considered a slave.

Emerson died in 1843, and three years later Scott sued Emerson's widow for his freedom. Scott won his case in a Missouri court in 1850, but in 1852 the State Supreme Court reversed the lower court's decision. Meanwhile, Mrs. Emerson remarried, and Scott became the legal property of her brother, John Sanford (misspelled as Sandford in court records). Scott sued Sanford for his freedom in federal court, and the court ruled against Scott in 1854.

When the case went to the Supreme Court, the justices ruled that Scott did not become a free man by virtue of having lived in a free state and that, as a black man, Scott was not a citizen and therefore was not entitled to bring suit in a court of law. The decision was widely criticized, and it contributed to the election of Abraham Lincoln, who opposed slavery, as president in 1860 and hastened the start of the Civil War in 1861. Dred Scott v. Sandford was overturned by the Thirteenth Amendment to the Constitution, which abolished slavery in 1865, and the Fourteenth Amendment, which granted citizenship to former slaves in 1868.

1878 – Reynolds v. United States – The Supreme Court upheld a federal law prohibiting polygamy (the system of marry marriages without terminating the previous ones) as correct.

1893 – Nix v. Hedden – Determined that a tomato was classified as a vegetable, not a fruit.

1896 – Plessy v. Ferguson – Supported the idea of "separate but equal" in relation to segregation.

1908 – Muller v. Oregon – In 1903, Oregon passed a law that women could work no more than ten hours a day in factories and laundries. A company called Muller's laundry required a woman to work more than ten hours, and Muller (the owner) was convicted of violating the law. He sued to appeal and was heard by the U.S. Supreme Court in 1908. The case of Muller v. Oregon questioned whether the Constitution permits states to pass laws to protect the health of workers. Oregon's attorney general assigned Louis D. Brandeis, a lawyer who supported reforms that protected workers, to defend the case. By a 9-0 vote, the justices upheld the Oregon law.

1919 – Schenck v. United States – Limited the right of freedom of speech by stating that those rights did not apply to speech which created a "clear and present danger."

1925 – Pierce v. Society of Sisters of the Holy Names of Jesus and Mary – Recognized that individuals have a right to privacy.

1925 – Gitlow v. New York – The fourteenth Amendment had a "due process" clause, which implies that no state shall deprive a person of life, liberty or properly without "due process" of law and the "equal protection" clause, which affirms that no state government shall deny any person equal protection of the laws. This was reflected in the Gitlow v. New York (1925) case wherein the Supreme Court held that the "…freedom of speech and the press, which are protected by the first amendment from abridgement by congress, are among the fundamental personal rights and liberties protected by the due process clause of the fourteenth amendment from impairment by the state…."

1937 – National Labor Relations Board (NLRB) v. Jones & Laughlin Steel Corp. – While Gibbons v. Ogden established the supremacy of Congress in regulating interstate commerce, NLRB v. Jones & Laughlin extended congressional authority from regulation of commerce itself to regulation of the business practices of industries that engage in interstate commerce.

Jones & Laughlin, one of the nation's largest steel producers, violated the National Labor Relations Act of 1935 by firing ten employees for engaging in union activities. The Act prohibited a variety of unfair labor practices and protected the rights of workers to form unions and to bargain collectively. The company refused to comply with an NLRB order to reinstate the workers. A Circuit Court of Appeals declined to enforce the board's order, and the Supreme Court reviewed the case.

A primary issue in this case was whether or not Congress had the authority to regulate the "local" activities of companies engaged in interstate commerce – that is, activities that take place within one state. Jones & Laughlin maintained that conditions in its factory did not affect interstate commerce and therefore were not under Congress's power to regulate. The Supreme Court disagreed, stating that "the stoppage of those [manufacturing] operations by industrial strife would have a most serious effect upon interstate commerce.... Experience has abundantly demonstrated that the recognition of the right of employees to self-organization and to have representatives of their own choosing for the purpose of collective bargaining is often an essential condition of industrial peace." By upholding the constitutionality of the National Labor Relations Act, the Supreme Court handed a victory to organized labor and set the stage for more far-reaching regulation of industry by the federal government.

1950 – Sweatt v. Painter – The court held that segregating black from white students is tantamount to preventing black students from interacting with whites, which is essential for a career in law.

1954 – Brown v. Board of Education of Topeka – Prior to this historic case, many states and the District of Columbia operated racially segregated school systems under the authority of the Supreme Court's 1896 decision in Plessy v. Ferguson, which allowed segregation if facilities were equal. In 1951 Oliver Brown of Topeka, Kansas, challenged this "separate-but-equal" doctrine when he sued the city school board on behalf of his eight-year-old daughter. Brown wanted his daughter to attend the white school that was five blocks from their home, rather than the black school that was twenty-one blocks away. Finding the schools substantially equal, a federal court ruled against Brown.

Meanwhile, parents of other black children in South Carolina, Virginia, and Delaware filed similar lawsuits. Delaware's court found the black schools to be inferior to white schools and ordered black children to be transferred to white schools, but school officials appealed the decision to the Supreme Court.

The Court heard arguments from all these cases at the same time. The briefs filed by the black litigants included data and testimony from psychologists and social scientists who explained why they thought segregation was harmful to black children. In 1954 a unanimous Supreme Court found that "...in the field of education the doctrine of 'separate but equal' has no place," and ruled that segregation in public schools denies black children "the equal protection of the laws guaranteed in the Fourteenth Amendment."

1957 – Roth v. United States – Determined that obscene material is not protected by the First Amendment.

1961 – Torcaso v. Watkins – Explained that the government cannot force a person to hold specific religious beliefs.

1962 – Baker v. Carr – Determined that reapportioning Congressional districts must be done in order to preserve the idea of "one man, one vote."

1962 – Engel v. Vitale – The Supreme Court affirmed that a nondenominational prayer composed by the New York Board of Regents for use in state public schools should not be used.

1964 – New York Times Co. v. Sullivan – The First Amendment to the U.S. Constitution guarantees freedom of the press, but for years the Supreme Court refused to use the First Amendment to protect the media from libel lawsuits – lawsuits based on the publication of false information that damages a person's reputation. The Supreme

Court's ruling in New York Times Co. v. Sullivan revolutionized libel law in the United States by deciding that public officials could not sue successfully for libel simply by proving that published information is false. The Court ruled that the complainant also must prove that reporters or editors acted with "actual malice" and published information "with reckless disregard of whether it was false or not."

The case arose from a full-page advertisement placed in the New York Times by the Southern Christian Leadership Conference to raise money for the legal defense of civil rights leader Martin Luther King, Jr., who had been arrested in Alabama in 1960. L.B. Sullivan, a city commissioner in Montgomery, Alabama, who was responsible for the police department, claimed that the ad libeled him by falsely describing the actions of the city police force. Sullivan sued the four clergymen who placed the ad and the New York Times, which had not checked the accuracy of the ad.

The advertisement did contain several inaccuracies, and a jury awarded Sullivan $500,000. The Times and the civil rights leaders appealed that decision to the Supreme Court, and the Court ruled unanimously in their favor. The Court decided that libel laws cannot be used "to impose sanctions upon expression critical of the official conduct of public officials," and that requiring critics to guarantee the accuracy of their remarks would lead to self-censorship. The Court found no evidence that the Times or the clergymen had malicious intent in publishing the ad.

1966 – Miranda v. Arizona – Clarence Earl Gideon was arrested for breaking into a poolroom in Florida in 1961. When he requested a court-appointed lawyer to defend him, the judge denied his plea, saying that state law required appointment of a lawyer only in capital cases – cases involving a person's death or calling for the death penalty. Gideon defended himself and was found guilty. While in prison, he spent hours in the library studying law books and handwriting a petition to the Supreme Court to hear his case. The Court decided that Gideon was denied a fair trial and ruled that every state must provide counsel for people accused of crimes who cannot afford to hire their own. When Gideon was retried with the help of a defense attorney, he was acquitted.

Just three years later the Supreme Court decided that the accused should have the right to counsel long before they get to a courtroom. Ernesto Miranda was convicted in a state court in Arizona of kidnapping and rape. His conviction was based on a confession Miranda gave to police officers after two hours of questioning, without being advised that he had the right to have an attorney present. In its ruling the Supreme Court required that police officers, when making arrests, must give what are now known as Miranda warnings – that suspects have the right to remain silent, that anything they say may be used against them, that they can have a lawyer present during questioning, and that a lawyer will be provided if they cannot afford one.

Miranda v. Arizona is one of the Supreme Court's best known decisions, as Miranda warnings are dramatized routinely in movies and television programs. However, in 1999 a Federal court of appeals challenged the decision in the case of Dickerson v. United States, in which a convicted bank robber claimed he had not been properly read his rights. In June 2000, the Supreme Court overturned Dickerson in a 7-2 ruling that strongly reaffirmed the validity of Miranda.

1969 – Tinker v. Des Moines Independent Community School District – Protected the free speech rights of students and teachers in public schools.

1969 – Brandenburg v. Ohio – Overturned the 1919 Schenck v. United States decision and stated instead that speech was protected by the First Amendment unless it represented "imminent lawless action."

1971 – Lemon v. Kurtzman – Established the Lemon Test which can be used to determine the constitutionality of acts related to education and religion.

1973 – Roe v. Wade – Determined that the government cannot restrict a woman's ability to get an abortion after the first trimester.

1989 – Texas v. Johnson – Gregory Lee Johnson doused an American flag with kerosene and set it on fire at a political demonstration in Texas, protesting the policies of the Reagan Administration and certain corporations based in Dallas. No one was hurt or threatened with injury, but Johnson was arrested. He was charged and convicted with the desecration of a venerated object, in violation of the Texas Penal Code. Johnson appealed in court, and in a split decision, the Supreme Court determined Johnson's actions to be symbolic speech protected by his First Amendment Rights. Congress passed the "Flag Protection Act" statute in 1989, making it a federal crime to desecrate the flag. In the case of United States v. Eichman in 1990, it was struck down by a five person majority of justices as in Johnson.

SACCO AND VENZETTI TRIAL

Fred Parmenter and Alessandro Berardelli, a paymaster and a security guard, were both were shot several times while moving the payroll boxes at their shoe company in South Braintree, Massachusetts. Two armed thieves (identified as "Italian-looking") fled in a Buick. The car was found abandoned in the woods several days later. Evidence found in the car led police to a man named Mike Boda, who fled to Italy. Police officers arrested Boda's colleagues, Nicola Sacco and Bartolomeo Vanzetti. After being tried and found guilty, Sacco and Vanzetti were executed in August 1927, but their conviction was controversial to the public.

During the trial, the prosecution's experts identified Sacco's gun as the murder weapon. The gun was the key evidence used to convict Sacco and Venzetti. The defense experts argued that the analysis of the evidence was crude, but on July 14, 1921, Sacco and Vanzetti were found guilty and sentenced to death. The ballistics issue refused to go away as Sacco and Vanzetti waited on death row. In 1927, Massachusetts Governor A. T. Fuller ordered another inquiry. Even though new and improved ballistics tests were ordered that proved beyond a doubt that Sacco's gun was the murder weapon, it was declared that Sacco and Vanzetti had not received a fair trial following the executions.

 Political Movements in the United States

Liberalism, Conservatism and Other Movements

The United States was conceived in the tradition of 18th century liberalism, a social and political set of values that decisively shaped our democratic politics. A political value system should be based on a belief in a government that has the full knowledge and approbation of all citizens being governed with the obligation to safeguard the rights, liberties and freedom in return for the citizens' absolute and unmitigated performance of their duties as citizens.

Eighteenth century Liberals were of the view that any given government derived the right to govern only on the basis of the said government's fulfilling its obligation to protect the just rights of the citizens. If such a government violates its obligation, the citizens have a right to oppose or resist or rebel against such a government. Earlier American settlers did exactly that against the British Empire. In the "Second Treatise of Civil Government," John Locke emphasized the concept of the free individual in the area of political realm, stating that the existence of government rests mainly on its safeguarding the natural rights of citizens.

Intellectually, there are two schools of thought, each opposing the other. One school thinks about "Liberalism" and the other enumerates "Conservatism." However, in essence, the U.S. political thought functions within the framework as well as parameters set out by the Founding Fathers of the nation. Conservatism follows with traditional liberal ideas, as it existed two hundred years ago. Ronald Reagan was a known conservative. All conservatives believe in free enterprise and commit themselves to capitalism. They would rather like to place the pecuniary resources of the nation in the hands of a few private individuals rather than striving to organize social programs effectively redistributing the wealth to the poor and downtrodden. They believe in the "magic of the marketplace" as Reagan said once. They strongly believe that a government should resist its temptation to interfere in the economic activities of the nation. They abhor too much power gradually accumulating to the government.

- President Franklin D. Roosevelt inherited a government that needed urgent economic restructuring as a result of the Great Depression. Nearly 33% of the people were found to be in abject poverty, most of them did not have a roof over their heads, were ill-clothed and mostly ill-fed. Roosevelt brought in the "New Deal" – a fitting economic and social reforms initiative. It was necessarily a new liberalism.
- A Conservative politician when in government would support personal life but oppose governmental intervention in business.
- A Liberal politician, on the other hand, would support government regulation of the economy as it has a close interaction as well as interdependence with societal wellbeing, but consider the personal life and morals the choice of an individual.
- Political thoughts of both conservatives and liberals have never been consistent in so far as their views and policies are concerned. While in government, conservatives were known to defend government subsidies to farmers, whereas liberals were found to bring in balanced budgets and reduced governmental spending.

For two hundred years and more, the U.S. democracy has survived many trials and tribulations and the main cause for this can be attributed to the liberal tradition and its underlying strengths.

ISOLATIONISM AND EXPANSIONISM

For most of history, the U.S. has followed a policy of isolation from global politics. Most Presidents as well as Congressmen preferred isolation. Europe at that time was riddled with cut-throat rivalries among nations and any U.S. entanglement in such a maze would only weaken the U.S. to a great extent. Although the U.S. followed a policy of isolation in the international arena, on the western hemisphere they were, to a very large extent, an expansionist power.

- Native Americans were engaged in frequent wars and were driven away from their traditional land.
- The "Monroe Doctrine," enunciated by President James Monroe advised the then European powers to keep from meddling in the Western Hemisphere. It also categorically spelled out the United States' right to supervise or manage political developments in North as well as South America.
- On May 13, 1846, the U.S. declared war on Mexico, which it ultimately won.
- The U.S. acquired colonies from the French, Spanish, and the Dutch.

Duty, dignity, discipline, liberty, equality, freedom of speech, freedom of religion, rule of law, and democratic values have always been influencing factors, motivating factors, in the U.S. expansionism.

 Demographics and Industry

DEMOGRAPHIC TRENDS

Demography encompasses the study of how human populations tend to change over a period of time. It deals, primarily, with the study and statistical arrangement of birth, death, marriage, divorce, migration, etc., happening in a particular region or area during a particular time. Demographic transition relates to the changes in population levels linked with economic development.

DEMOGRAPHIC VARIABLES

To determine trends in population, three variables are taken into account.

1. Fertility rate
2. Mortality
3. Migration rate

They are also referred to as

1. Crude birth rate, i.e., the annual birth rate per 1000 people.
2. Crude death rate, i.e., the annual death rate per 1000 people.
3. Net migration rate; i.e. the net difference between people coming into a given population of 1000 and those who move out of it.

IMMIGRANTS

The United States of America is the primary choice for immigrants, world over. No other nation has ever admitted immigrants in such numbers. In fact, the U.S. admits more immigrants than all the other countries put together.

NATURE OF WORK

In the year 1776, when the nation was born, almost ninety-one percent of the people of the colonies were farmers. Agriculture was mainly pursued as a means of livelihood. Many colonies engaged in labor. In the Southern Colonies, tobacco was the major crop and the slave trade thrived there.

Other occupations during the colonial period were fishing, whaling, lumber felling and shaping/sizing, and fur-trapping. Slowly, the colonists found that the abundant supply of wood in the innumerable forests surrounding them was a rich material for ship-building. The American ship-building method turned out to be cheaper than the

European methods. Iron-products, hats, woolen and textile goods, glass, stoneware pottery, alcoholic beverages were also made in colonies. Professions such as carpentry, black smithy, weaving, and handicrafts slowly found their footing.

The war of 1812, fought against England, saw the stoppage of exports for three years of English goods. This prompted growth in the colonies as they had to build their own factories. Cotton and woolen mills thrived. The American Civil War saw the government buying a good quantity of firearms, clothing, and foodstuff. This had become the necessary fillip for large-scale industrialization.

The agricultural economy gave way to an industrial economy and World Wars I and II saw the U.S. becoming a super economic and technological power. Then came the information explosions, which lead to America becoming a knowledge economy.

From its beginnings as primarily a farmer's society, the U.S. had become an industrial, knowledge-based society with every occupation under the sun having the highest skills. Today, the SOHO – small office/home office – segment is thriving, thanks to information as well as the Internet revolution. Over the years the nature of work has changed from basically hard physical labor to that of highly skilled mental work.

TRIANGLE SHIRTWAIST FIRE

The Triangle Waist Company, one of the largest blouse makers in New York City, was owned by Max Blanck and Isaac Harris. They specialized in making shirtwaists, a very popular women's blouse that had a tight waist and puffy sleeves. Approximately 500 people, mostly immigrant women and many of them young, worked there six days a week. Space was cramped, working conditions were poor, and they earned low wages.

Near closing time on March 25, 1911, a fire broke out at the Triangle Waist Factory in New York City. Within eighteen minutes, 146 people were dead as a result of the fire. Workers attempted to put it out with the fire hoses, but no water came out. The elevators quickly filled to thirty - double their capacity. After only a few trips the fire reached the elevator shafts as well. About twenty people made it down the fire escape before the stairs collapsed, killing twenty-five others. Many on the tenth floor, including Blanck and Harris, made it safely to the roof and then were helped to nearby buildings. However, those on the eighth and ninth floors were stuck. The fire was put out in thirty minutes.

Blanck and Harris were tried for manslaughter, but were found not guilty. The incident revealed the hazardous conditions these high-rise factories had. Shortly after the Triangle fire, New York City passed a large number of fire, safety, and building codes.

NORTHERN SECURITIES CASE

The Northern Securities Case was Roosevelt's first of use of anti-trust legislation to dismantle a monopoly. In 1901, railroad builder James J. Hill and his rival Edward H. Harriman fought for control of the Chicago, Burlington, and Quincy Railroad. Hill, who controlled the Great Northern and the Northern Pacific railroads, wanted access to Chicago for his lines from the Twin Cities. After an extended bidding war for the CB&Q, Hill and Harriman instead created the Northern Securities Company, aided by banker J. P. Morgan and financier John D. Rockefeller. Established in the state of New Jersey (which had laws favorable to this type of arrangement), Northern Securities held the majority of railroad shares from Chicago to the Pacific Northwest.

In 1902, Roosevelt instructed the Justice Department to break up this holding company on the grounds that it was acting in restraint of trade. Northern Securities sued to appeal the ruling. The Supreme Court heard the case in 1904, ruling 5-4 in favor of the federal government.

Roosevelt's action established his reputation as a "trust buster." This increased his popular support, and helped in his election campaign in 1904.

UNIONS

Eugene v. Debs (1855-1926) was a labor organizer and socialist leader. In 1893 he became President of the American Railway Union. In 1894, the ARU conducted a successful strike against the Great Northern Railway for higher wages. After playing a leading role in the Chicago Pullman Palace Car Company strike, he was sent to jail. Between 1900 and 1920, Debs was the Socialist party's standard-bearer in five presidential elections. Between campaigns, he was a tireless speaker and organizer for the Socialist party. He traveled the nation defending workers in their strikes and industrial disputes. Many workers applauded his vision, but few endorsed his political program.

The fact remains that not more than twenty percent of the working class are members of the Trade Unions today. Even during the 1950's when trade unionism was at its peak trade union membership did not cross the 25% mark. The oldest organization, in fact it was established in the year 1886, was the American Federation of Labor (AFL). From 1930 onwards the Congress of Industrial Organization (CIO) came into the limelight.

Rapid industrialization saw to its growth. In 1955, the AFL merged with the CIO to form AFL-CIO, which became labor's most prominent support organization. The AFL-CIO guides policies on the macro-level i.e., policies relating to labor as a whole in so far as minimum wages, occupational health and safety, consumer protection, the tax code, job training, employment and social welfare are concerned, leaving the micro-level, i.e., a particular unit's local problems, to the concerned member organizations.

COMMON OCCUPATIONS

In America, the leading occupations are:

(1) Professional and related jobs
(2) Service
(3) Management, business and financial
(4) Construction and extraction
(5) Installation, maintenance and repair
(6) Transportation and material moving
(7) Sales, marketing and related
(8) Office and administrative support
(9) Farming, fishing and forestry
(10) Production

Social Growth of America

IMMIGRATION AND THE HISTORY OF RACIAL MINORITIES

The first Americans were the Native American tribes. To date there is no clear knowledge about how or when they came to North America. There is a school of thought which earnestly believe that the Indian had crossed over from Asia on the land mass that was believed to have connected Siberia and Alaska, probably some thirty to forty thousand years ago! When Columbus fortuitously landed in America, there were already half a million Indians in the areas later known as the United States.

Thousands of African slaves were brought in chains by the English traders to be sold in the New World. The Colonial South with its innumerable tobacco plantations and rice fields was the primary motivation for slave ships to import a huge slave population to work in the field. The North always was against slavery, but even in the northern states, after slaves were freed, they did face economic, social as well as educational discrimination.

The people who came and settled before the American Revolution came to be known as "Colonists." Those who came afterwards were called "Immigrants." Both "Colonists" and "Immigrants" mostly hailed from Europe.

Most of them came to the brave New World in search of riches and happiness that they could not obtain in their own country of origin. Between 1830 and 1930, it was estimated that there arrived thirty-seven million immigrants into the U.S. Until 1890, the immigrants were primarily from Europe, i.e., from England, Ireland, France, Germany and the Scandinavian countries. After 1890, most new immigrants were from Italy,

Austria, Greece, Russia, Poland and Hungary. Immigrants faced hostility from already settled people.

The Alien and Sedition Acts of 1798 sought to resist Irish and French immigrants. The Ku Klux Klan showered hostility on foreigners in the 1920's. In the 1950's people feared that the new immigrants were bringing in communist ideals.

In essence, the United States of America was created "out of many, one" as states the Latin phrase "E Pluribus Unum" on the Great Seal of United States!

FREEDOM SUMMER OF 1964

In 1964, civil rights organizations including CORE, COFO, and SNCC organized a voter registration drive called the Mississippi Summer Project, or Freedom Summer. Freedom Summer was part of a larger effort by civil rights activists aimed at increasing the black vote registration. In 1962, less than 7 percent of the state's eligible black voters were registered to vote.

The Freedom Summer faced constant abuse and harassment from Mississippi's white population and the Ku Klux Klan, including arson, beatings, false arrest and the murder of at least three civil rights activists. The Mississippi project registered twelve hundred African-Americans and established fifty Freedom Schools to carry on community organizing.

URBANIZATION

During the early colonial period, and even after the birth of the nation, the vast majority of people were engaged in agriculture and farm-related production. Though agriculture was the main occupation of many, fishing, whaling, fur-tapping, timber cutting, shipping and making products also thrived. People, normally, lived in village clusters near their farmlands.

There were no paved roads, not much industrial activity and therefore there was no urbanization. Only after 1812, during the war with the British in which England prohibited exports from the British Isles or its other colonies to the United States, did the idea of industrializing occur. Cotton and woolen mills sprung up everywhere.

By 1815, the U.S. had six times as many cotton spindles working compared to the beginning of the War of 1812. From 1812 to 1861, American industry grew at a snail's pace due to British goods, more especially in the textiles sector, being superior and cheaper and, therefore, they could not be outsold by the imitation American products.

By 1860, the U.S. had established the largest railroad system in the world connecting almost all parts of the country. In fact the U.S. had more railroads than all of Europe combined. The government bought abundant foodstuff, clothing, war equipment and firearms during the Civil War, which served as a catalyst for huge industrial investment. Until 1860 nearly fifty percent of Americans were involved in farming but after a 100 years only about six percent were employed in agricultural farming.

The California Gold Rush of 1849 brought people in huge numbers who spread out from the Mississippi River to California. The Northeast had seaports, which helped commerce to a great extent. It also had growing cities. Textile mills, shoe and other footwear factories, dairies which also turned out other dairy products were established.

Mines were dug and more and more factories producing very many different products were established. More farming came into being. More people came to settle in the emerging most prosperous country in the world. A proactive government which fixed a high tariff on foreign imports made U.S. products cheaper and hence consumption of all-American products increased by leaps and bounds. From 1900 onwards more time and money were spent on building highways, buildings, etc., which made urbanization easier.

There came a few men who became captains of industry:

John D. Rockefeller organized the standard oil company.
Cyrus McCormick built fast working farm machines.
Andrew Carnegie built a steel empire, in which, at one time, more than 40 millionaires worked.

By 1927, there were as many as forty-four automobile firms in the country. Corporate business houses became larger and larger. Automation took control of larger factories. Bigger cities came into being abutting what were once green field factories. Computers came on the scene, a move which brought in its wake a veritable information explosion. The Internet revolution changed everything!

Today, any sort of information on any part of the world is available at the push of a button. Lifestyle changed. People started living in luxurious homes. Skyscrapers came into being. Technological innovations even saw the U.S. sending a man to the moon.

GROWTH OF CITIES

Even in 3500 B.C., cities on a larger scale existed. Rome, it was estimated, had more than a million inhabitants when it was at its peak.

What is a city? A city is a place where a large number of inhabitants live permanently. They don't produce their own food but work in factories, or offices for a living. This has become possible only because of Industrialization. Larger cities are called "metropolises."

The Twelve Fastest and Slowest Growing U.S. Cities			
Fastest		Slowest	
1. Las Vegas, NV	26.2%	Salinas, CA	-1.1%
2. McAllen, TX	20.2	Brighamton, NY	-1.0
3. Boise City, ID	17.5	Scranton, PA	-0.2
4. Bremerton, WA	16.2	Jersey City, NJ	-0.1
5. Olympia, WA	16.1	Utica, NY	-0.1
6. Brownsville, TX	15.2	Pittsburgh, PA	0.3
7. Colorado Springs, CO	14.0	New York, NY	0.4
8. Austin, TX	13.9	Bridgeton, NJ	0.5
9. Atlanta, GA	12.6	Dayton, OH	0.5
10. Killeen, TX	12.5	Philadelphia, PA	0.5
11. Knoxville, TN	12.5	Shreveport, LA	0.5
12. El Paso, TX	12.4	Youngstown, OH	0.5

Note: Percentage of population charge 1990-1994. A minus sign indicates a loss of population.

AT 12.4 Raleigh, NC ties El Paso, but lost out due to alphabetizing

When the United States was founded, it was mostly an agriculture economy, and therefore, had a rural existence. The change to urbanization has been gradual. Today about eighty percent of Americans live in cities. The U.S. Census Bureau has divided the country into 269 MSA's (Metropolitan Statistical Areas). Each and every MSA comprises a central city and the urbanized country areas linked to it.

THE CHANGING NATURE OF AGRICULTURAL LIFE

Early colonists had no other alternative except producing their own agricultural products for a living. This trend continued till the 1812 War with the British. At that time, more than ninety percent of the people worked in farms. They lived in a rural setting. There were no highways or railroads. They used horse-driven or ox-driven carts on makeshift rough roads for conveyance and goods carriage. There were clusters of homes near their farmlands. They produced wheat, rice, barley, corn, oats, and rye in the New England areas.

In southern colonies, more especially in the Virginia region, they produced tobacco, a cash crop, which brought them prosperity. The colonists, being mostly raw hands and new to agriculture, did not have the skills required nor the equipment and implements to till the soil. Naturally, they had to work for rich landlords in return for feeding their family and keeping hunger at bay. Even if there was a bumper harvest, there were not many buyers to purchase it. Tobacco, of course, brought them money.

They exported their produce to Europe on a regular business process. Most of the people lived in penury, ill health and squalor. Tobacco plantations needed a large work force, which resulted in the slave trade. The conditions in which slaves lived were even worse. They were segregated and treated like animals. Pennsylvania received wealthy immigrants. Prisoners were brought in as workers. Tobacco plantations were taking root in the southern parts of the U.S. and the liquor business grew. Then the inventions on cotton ginning gave a new fillip to cotton production. Production of mechanized agricultural equipment doubled agricultural production and created new employment opportunities. Gradually the conditions and lifestyle improved. There was a veritable green revolution. The export of agricultural products to Europe brought in prosperity.

ECONOMIC GROWTH AND DEVELOPMENT

The War of 1812 saw goods from England to the United States drying up. It had become imperative for Americans to build their own factories and make inventions and innovations in manufacture, management and technology. There were many, many woolen and cotton mills by 1815.

The peace between England and America slowed down the growth. But after the Civil War a veritable revolution – the Industrial Revolution – took America by storm. The telegraph, electric bulb, railroads, printing machinery, typewriter, telephone exchange, mechanized agricultural equipment, etc., were all invented.

The social fabric of the United States gradually marched towards industrialization and hence there was a veritable population shift from rural to urban cities.

ECONOMIC FABRIC

From 1776 when more than ninety percent of the people of the country depended mainly on agriculture, to the present day, where the U.S. is rated to be the Super Economic Power, the march has been arduous; single minded devotion, hard work and a spirit of innovation garnered exceptional advancement in the areas of industry, commerce, and, trade.

- In 1793, Eli Whitney invented the Cotton Gin, revolutionizing the cotton industry.
- In 1704, the Boston News Letter, the world's first newspaper, was launched in Boston.
- In 1844, Samuel Morse's telegraphic codes were firmly established between America and England.

- Between 1861 and 1865, railroads were built connecting all parts of the United States. Industries and business developed in cities.
- In 1868 the typewriter was invented.
- In 1876 Alex and Graham Bell's telephone was patented. In 1878, the first Telephone Exchange was built in New Haven.
- In 1882 the first electric bulb was invented.

All these inventions brought excellent returns to the United States. Industry and Commerce leaped to new heights. Imports and exports scaled new heights. Today the U.S.A. is the world's leading industrialized nation. Approximately sixty percent of the manufacturing activity lies in the States east of the Mississippi River and north of the Ohio River.

INDUSTRIAL GROWTH

In 1877, Rutherford B. Hayes became President. A vast industrial and business expansion took place. The next thirty years saw the establishing of 400,000 kilometers of railroad. Telephone and telegraph systems were established and a new faster method of printing took shape. North Dakota, South Dakota, Washington and Montana joined the Union. Cities were growing rapidly. Immigrants in the millions came to share the prosperity. In 1912, Woodrow Wilson, a democrat, became President. He created new banking and currency systems controlled by the Federal Reserve Board. The Clayton Act regulated trusts. The Federal Trade Commission was established. The 16th Amendment was passed which made it possible for federal income tax. Wilson also lowered duties through legislation. In 1913, World War I broke out in Europe. War had made the U.S. an arsenal of the most sophisticated weaponry. Its air power as well as sea power was awesome. World War I had seen the birth of a super power.

The 1920s are considered as a prosperous decade. Skyscrapers were built. There was a general boom all-round. Schools, colleges and universities expanded. President Hoover took office in 1929. By October, the Stock Market crashed. The United States was pulled into the world wide Depression steadily. Industries came to a grinding halt in the wake of total financial breakdown. Unemployment soared. Hoover failed. In 1933, Franklin Delano Roosevelt, a democrat, became President. His "New Deal" was considered exemplary. His moves tied down a further sliding of the economy, and He won re-election decisively. He scrapped prohibition. The Second World War saw the U.S. producing planes, ships, guns and other war-related products at a frenetic pace. On August 6, 1945, the first Nuclear Bomb was dropped on the city of Hiroshima, evaporating the city in seconds.

On July 1969, Apollo-II mission's astronauts landed on the moon. The Watergate scandal broke out. Inflation, unemployment, recession, stagnation continued from Nixon's tenure into Ford's. By early 1980, the U.S. had come under the grip of a mild recession. Ronald Reagan became President in 1980. He got the U.S. embassy hostages in Iran released. Unemployment figures almost touched double figures. He authored the S.D.I. (Strategic Defense Initiative) to safeguard men and material of the U.S. from foreign attack. Reagan's term had the dubious distinction of increasing the national debt from 914 billion to over 2.5 trillion. By the middle of 1990, the recession began to show its ugly face yet again.

In 1992, Bill Clinton, a Democrat, won the Presidency. The North American free trade agreement between the U.S.A., Canada and Mexico was signed. A deficit reduction passage and a family lease act were passed. In 1996, Clinton was reelected. The economy during his tenure was strong and continued to grow during his second innings also. In 1999, the U.S. registered the largest budget surpluses in the history of the nation. George W. Bush, son of the former President George Bush, became President. He brought in a 1.35 trillion dollar Tax-Cut Bill which became law in June 2001.

Today, the U.S. is the most advanced economy of the world. By sheer hard work and visionary zeal, the country of many immigrants has become the most acclaimed country in the world.

TRENDS IN WOMEN AND THE FAMILY

Women, traditionally, were taking on more responsibilities in a family set-up. Men have always been dominant in any society in the world. Today women are the most independent, creative, well organized, educated, and most aspiring section of society, compared to a majority of countries. They work in factories, offices, or government offices for eight hours a day or more, and then come home and take care of children, and attend to daily household chores for another six to eight hours a day.

U.S. women have acquired dignity and respectability only through continued striving. From time immemorial, western societies were known to be patriarchal. Male dominance in society has long been established and proper roles for women have been earmarked. Women were, normally, relegated to rear and nurture children and take full care of home maintenance.

Slowly this has changed over the years in the U.S. after a step-by-step struggle for total freedom. Today women work shoulder to shoulder with men in almost every field. They fought for the Equal Rights Amendment through feminist Alice Paul. (Proposed by Alice Paul in the year 1923 this act got Congressional approbation not until 1972.) In 1960's the Equal Pay act of 1963 got them equal pay as men. Title VII of the Civil Rights Act of 1964 gained prohibition of sexual discrimination.

In the year 1972, Title VII of the Civil Rights Act of 1964 was extended to educational institutions under Title IX. Women fought for 'Women's Suffrage' through The Grimke sisters of Charleston, South Carolina. Angelina Grimke said in 1836: "…. Human beings have rights, because they are moral beings: the rights of all men grew out of the moral nature, and as all men have the same moral nature, they have essentially the same rights….. Now, if rights are founded in the nature of our moral being, then the mere circumstance of sex does not give man higher rights and responsibilities, than to a woman…" It took a long time for women to get voting rights – in fact they were given that right only in August 1920, almost eighty years after the Grimke sisters fought for it.

Today, the women's workforce is larger than that of men. In the year 1900, only twenty percent of workers were women. By 1940, they had become twenty-five percent and by 1960, thirty-three percent. Today, women comprise almost fifty percent of the workforce.

1. Of the 115 million women of age 16 years and over in the U.S., 68 million are labor force participants – working or looking for work.
2. With a labor force participation rate of 59.5 percent, women represent 47 percent of the total U. S. labor force.
3. Labor force participation rates for women, by race, are: black, 61.9 percent; white, 59.2 percent; Asian, 58.3 percent; and Hispanic, 55.9 percent.
4. Women are projected to comprise forty-seven percent of the total labor force in 2013 as they did in 2003. They will also account for fifty-five percent of the increase in the total labor force growth from 2002-2013.
5. The higher a person's educational attainment, the more likely they will be a labor force participant. Here are the labor force participation rates for women of age twenty-five years and over by educational attainment: with less than a high school diploma – 32.7 percent; with a high school diploma – 55.0 percent; some college, no degree – 64.8 percent; associate degree – 71.8; and bachelor's degree and higher – 73.1 percent.
6. Greater educational attainment usually results in lower unemployment rates: women with less than a high school diploma – 9.8 percent; with a high school diploma – 5.2 percent; some college, no degree – 4.9 percent; and bachelor's degree and higher – 2.9 percent.
7. There were 64.4 million employed women in the U.S. in 2003. Seventy-four percent worked full time, while the remaining twenty-six percent worked part time.
8. The largest percentage of employed women (thirty-eight percent) worked in management, professional, and related occupations, while thirty-five percent worked in sales and office occupations.
9. Smaller percentages worked in service occupations, twenty percent; seven percent worked in production, transportation, and material moving occupations; and one percent worked natural resources, construction, and maintenance occupations.
10. Approximately 4 million women were self-employed in non-agricultural industries. These self-employed women represented nearly six percent of all employed women.

11. The seven occupations with the highest median weekly earnings among women who worked full-time in 2003 were: lawyers, $1,413; pharmacists, $1,364; computer and information systems managers, $1,280; chief executives, $1,243; computer software engineers, $1,005; physicians and surgeons, $989; and management analysts, $977.

Still work place harassment and sexual abuse persist but to a lesser degree compared to the previous century.

Women are the main axis around which every family revolves. Every civilization and every human group throughout the world organizes its members only in families. In the broader sense, a family is an amalgamation of a husband, a wife and child or children, living as unit. A nuclear family consists of a husband, wife and children whereas an extended family consists, in addition to the members of a nuclear family, others like grandparents, uncles and cousins who also form a part in the enlarged unit. A marriage can be considered as a social license, having the wholehearted approbation of the family unit, for mating. A family is universal because it seeks to fulfill basic criteria for a given society's wellbeing. The criteria are:

(1) Economic aspects
(2) Caring for the sick and aged
(3) Reproduction
(4) Socialization of children
(5) Recreation

PHYLLIS SCHLAFLY

A strong advocate of conservative rights, Phyllis Schlafly is a woman best known for her opposition to the Equal Rights Amendment in the 1970's. Phyllis was born in St Louis in 1924 and earned a Master's degree from Radcliffe College in Massachusetts and later a law degree from Washington University Law School in St Louis.

In 1952, she ran for Congress and although she was unsuccessful, she stayed active in politics. In 1964, she entered the political scene again by writing a book called A Voice Not An Echo which advocated the presidential nomination of a conservative candidate. In the 1970's when the Equal Rights Amendment was proposed, she took action and wrote an article called *What's Wrong with the Equal Rights Amendment*, which quickly gained the approval of conservatives across the nation. She organized rallies, baked bread for legislators, and appeared on television - all in an effort to prevent the passage of the amendment. The purpose of the Equal Rights Amendment was to make it illegal to discriminate on a basis of gender. She argued that the amendment would destroy conservative family values and would strongly disadvantage full time homemakers. Due in large part to her efforts, the bill was never passed.

EMMA GOLDMAN

Emma Goldman (1869-1940) was an anarchist who struggled for decades against inequality, repression and exploitation. She was an advocate of freedom of expression, sexual freedom and birth control, equality and independence for women, radical education, union organization and workers' rights. Her deep commitment to the ideal of absolute freedom led her to these causes. Support for these controversial ideas earned Goldman the enmity of powerful political and economic authorities.

She became known as "exceedingly dangerous," was often harassed or arrested while lecturing, and sometimes banned outright from speaking. Goldman, determined to express herself, became a prominent figure in the establishment of the right to freedom of speech in America.

THE BOY SCOUTS

The Boy Scouts of America organization was founded in 1910 by William D. Boyce, Ernest Thompson Seton, Daniel Carter Beard, Lord Robert Baden-Powell. The goal of the organization is to support young people in their physical, mental and spiritual development so they may play constructive roles in society, with a strong focus on the outdoors and survival skills. Today it is one of the largest youth organizations in the United States. The Boy Scouts of America believes in shaping the future by helping today's youth, creating a more conscientious, responsible, and productive society. Scouting is designed to meet six needs for young people: mentoring, lifelong learning, faith traditions, serving others, healthy living, and character building. They combine educational activities, lifelong values, and fun.

SCOPES TRIAL

In 1925 in Tennessee a biology teacher named John Scopes was sued for teaching evolution, a scientific idea which contrasts with the creation story of the Bible. He was represented by a very famous attorney, Clarence Darrow and was prosecuted by three time presidential candidate William Jennings Bryan.

Two quotations from the trial have since become famous:

I do not consider it an insult, but rather a compliment to be called an agnostic. I do not pretend to know where many ignorant men are sure — that is all that agnosticism means.

If today you can take a thing like evolution and make it a crime to teach it in the public school, tomorrow you can make it a crime to teach it in the private schools, and the next year you can make it a crime to teach it to the hustings or in the church. At the next session you may ban books and the newspapers. Soon you may set Catholic against Protestant and Protestant against Protestant, and try to foist your own religion upon the minds of men. If you can do one you can do the other. Ignorance and fanaticism is ever busy and needs feeding. Always it is feeding and gloating for more. Today it is the public school teachers, tomorrow the private. The next day the preachers and the lectures, the magazines, the books, the newspapers. After a while, your honor, it is the setting of man against man and creed against creed until with flying banners and beating drums we are marching backward to the glorious ages of the sixteenth century when bigots lighted fagots to burn the men who dared to bring any intelligence and enlightenment and culture to the human mind.

He was convicted and fined $100 but the ruling was later overturned on a technicality. The event started a shift in opinions away from fundamentalism, the practice of teaching things according to the Bible.

C. WRIGHT MILLS

C. Wright Mills (1916-1962) was an influential sociologist in the early 1900's. He is most well-known for two of his books: The Power Elite (1956) and The Sociological Imagination (1959). In The Power Elite, Mills makes the argument that there is no such thing as true democracy in the United States due to a formation of an elite hierarchy. He argued that certain key people in government, military, and the corporate world held the majority of influence and authority that left the average citizen with little power. Mills was very concerned about what he considered to be the loss of a middle class. He placed a significant importance on knowledge as a means of bringing about change, and felt that that knowledge could be obtained through critical thinking. In his book The Sociological Imagination Mills identifies biography, social structure, and history as three elements of "Sociological Imagination" which allows an individual to look beyond their personal environment and concerns to see the bigger picture of the society and enable themselves to find solutions.

Major Movements of the Arts

PAINTING AND SCULPTURES

There are thousands of professional painters, sculptors and other artists in today's U.S. Every year about 1,000 arts schools turn out appropriately one quarter of a million artists. There are hundreds of art museums throughout the U.S. exhibiting some of the finest and most well-known works of famous artists.

The tastes of artists differ. Each artist, throughout history, has brought in new ideas, aesthetic values, alluring expressions and color codes and more. In the 19th century, Impressionism was the movement favored by French Artists such as Monet, Renoir, and Degas. An American artist, Mary Canatt followed impressionists' ideas.

Abstract Expressionism is considered an American movement based mostly on the lines of European Abstraction and Surrealism. It was the "in" thing in the 1940's. Legor, Hans Hoffman, Max-Ernst, Arshile Gorky who came to America during the World War II period were Artists of the Abstract Expressionist genre. Jackson Pollock, Mark Rothko, Barnett Newman as well as William de Kooning were well known American Abstract Expressionists. Geometric abstraction, drip paintings, field paintings using soft color were some of the styles of the artists mentioned. Sculptors like Reuben Nakian followed abstract Expressionism. Famous Artist Van Gogh was considered to be a forerunner of the Abstract Expressionist Movement.

Pop Art is an American Art Movement practiced in the 1950's and 1960's. Andy Warhol, Robert Rauchenberg and Jasper Johns were the first followers of Pop Art. The underlying theme of Pop Art has been painting emotions in a somber, cool genre as opposed to depicting emotion as strong as possible in Abstract Expressionism. The artist's personality remains outside the art in Pop Art whereas in Abstract Expressionism, the artist's individualism shines through the canvas. Claes Oldenburg is considered a Pop-Art sculptor.

Op Art was an unorganized artists' movement of the 1960's. It emphasizes the optical effects on canvas as well as the mingling effects of colors and hues. If one wants to create an optical illusion, "opt for Op Art" is the refrain of Artists. Josef Albers and Victor Vasarley are two of the best known Op Artists.

Environmental Art (a.k.a. Earth Art) was a movement of the 1970's depicting nature as the backdrop of content. This art form is mainly individualistic. By nature such arts are poetic and conceptual. Christo; Jeanney Claude, Robert Smithson and Spiral Jelty are known Earth Artists.

Conceptual Art is a late 20th century art using many forms as well as mediums to portray forceful ideas in a realistic way. Ann Hamilton and Christian Boltanski are considered conceptual artists.

Installation forms of art create larger than life three-dimensional gatherings of forms and objects, utilizing a large space. Art Kienholz is known to be the first Installation artist, and George Segal is also known to be an Installation Artist. He used to mold real people using plaster of Paris. Judy Pfaff is considered to be a sculptor who uses Installation Art in the themes. Kerry James Marshall, an African American, is considered an

Installation Artist. Maya Lin is a sculptor/architect who designed the Vietnam memorial in Washington.

"American Gothic" is a painting and a touchstone of American culture. It depicts an older man and woman in front of their home, with the man holding a pitchfork. The painter, Grant Wood, was born in Iowa. Between 1920 and 1926, Wood traveled through Europe, and some of his artistic style is attributed to the 15th century realism and artistry he viewed there. When he returned to Iowa, he was appreciative of Midwestern traditions and culture, which he celebrated in his works. Wood and his paintings were rooted in the Midwest. American Gothic can be seen as a comment on Midwestern character, or as a statement about rural American values, an image of reassurance with the man and woman, in their solid and well-crafted world, representing survivors.

LITERATURE

During the early Colonial period, Captain John Smith (1580-1631) published an account of his experiences in the Jamestown Settlement, and called it "A True Relation of Occurrences and Accidents in Virginia."

William Bradford (1590-1657) described the Pilgrims Journey in History of Plymouth Plantation (1856). The Puritans wrote prolifically.

Uncle Tom's Cabin by Harriet Beecher Stowe was a trailblazer.

Horace Mann, Charles Finney, Henry Thoreau, Ralph Waldo Emerson as well as Theodore Parker were thinkers who contributed liberally to American culture.

Louis Clark's History (1814) and Washington Irving's History of New York (1809) ushered the U.S. into the literary garden. Irving's Rip Van Winkle created a literary awakening.

Fennimore Cooper's novel The Spy (1821) was an exciting thriller.

The greatest Southern writer was Edgar Allen Poe (1809-49) who wrote many books such as The Fall of the House of Usher, William Wilson, and The Pit and the Pendulum.

Herman Melville (1819-91) published Moby Dick.

Pearl S. Buck's book The Good Earth won her the Nobel Prize.

Samuel Langhorne Clemens – (a.k.a. Mark Twain) (1835-1910) was one of the best Humorists of the time wrote The Adventures of Tom Sawyer (1876), The Prince and the Pauper (1882), and The Adventures of Huckleberry Finn (1884).

Another humorist, P.G. Wodehouse (the creator of the character "Jeeves") enthralled millions by his witty writing.

There were others like Robert Frost and Emily Dickinson who contributed to the literary scene liberally. Lew Wallace's "Ben-Hur" enthralled millions. The poetry of Thomas Stearns Eliot is both traditional and modern.

Gone with the Wind was written by Margaret Mitchell in 1936. The story is set in Georgia during the Civil War. In the book, Scarlett O'Hara antagonizes her community with her own determination and lack of scruples in her drive to acquire money. Her careless behavior in toying with people turns everybody against her, and she is left ultimately friendless and loveless after suffering a great deal of loss. Gone with the Wind was Mitchell's only novel, but it was immediately popular. It was at the top of the American fiction bestseller list the year it was published. More than 30 million copies have been printed worldwide. Mitchell received the Pulitzer Prize for Fiction in 1937. It was adapted to a film in 1939.

Catcher in the Rye was written by J. D. Salinger in 1951. The story is narrated by Holden Caulfield. Undergoing treatment in a mental hospital, he narrates events that take place between the end of the fall school term and Christmas, when he is sixteen years old. Symbolism is found all throughout the novel, such as in Holden's red hunting hat which represents his love for everything with unusual, people and objects alike. Allie's baseball mitt represents Holden's love for his brother. The rings on the carousel represent hopes, dreams and the fact that we must take chances to grab them. Holden wishes to "catch" the children who are playing in the rye field if they fall of the cliff (from childhood to adulthood - protecting their innocence).

Sylvia Plath lived from 1932-1963. She wrote well-crafted poems that were very personal known as "confessional poetry." She also wrote The Bell Jar which was a novel loosely based on her life. She suffered from depression and committed suicide in 1963.

NONFICTION LITERATURE

Rachel Carson was a marine biologist who wrote the book Silent Spring and The Sea Around Us which significantly impacted and furthered the environmental movement.

Ralph Nader wrote a book about automobile safety called Unsafe at Any Speed in 1965. He advocated for the use of safety equipment in cars, such as seat belts. This was his first book resulting in his name becoming famous.

Dr. Benjamin Spock (May 2, 1903-March 15, 1998) was a pediatrician. He published the highly successful book Common Sense Book of Baby and Child Care. He urged parents to trust their common sense, be flexible, and refrain from using corporal punishment. The book has been published in 39 languages and sold over 50 million copies. Spock and his manual helped revolutionize child-rearing methods for the post-World War II generation. Spock emphasizes in his book that, above all, parents should have confidence in their abilities and trust their instincts. The famous first line of the book reads, "Trust yourself. You know more than you think you do."

THEATER

Arthur Miller wrote <u>Death of Salesman</u> in 1949 which won the Pulizer Prize for best drama and several Tony Awards. This powerful drama examines deep conflict in an immediate family and the changing social norms for the middle class. The main character Willy is a failed salesman, having an affair, unhappy with his job and losing his touch on reality. He is disappointed in his children who have not "made something" of themselves. After several arguments and plot complications, the play ends with Willy committing suicide and leaving the life insurance money to his son to start his own business.

FILM

Rebel Without a Cause is a 1955 American drama film. In the story, a rebellious teenager named Jim arrives at a new high school, meets a girl, disobeys his parents, and defies the school bully. It uses a variety of tools (such as the plot, color, bullets, a jacket, and more) to be symbolic of the current social and political climate. Cold War symbolism is woven into the plot. An example of this is the fight between Jim and the bully, symbolic of the macho struggle of the Cold War. The "chicken game" they play shows the need to show they are the bigger power. Eventually, the challenge leads to the bully's death. Another theme of the movie is the generational difference between the kids and their parents, shown by how the children frequently disobey their parents. *Rebel Without a Cause* also shows the dynamics of an American nuclear family.

ARCHITECTURE

Frank Lloyd Wright was an internationally acclaimed architect known for his work to create a distinctly "American" style of architecture. He was born and attended school in Wisconsin. After studying civil engineering for two years at the University of Wisconsin, Wright moved to Chicago to work for an architect named Joseph Silsbee. Later in his career, Wright credited Silsbee as his primary mentor. Wright felt that architecture should be a matter of "Form and Function." He argued that rather than simply constructing buildings after the same European styles, that design should primarily consider functionality. His style became known for be unique and organic. His most famous works were his own home named Taliesin, a beautiful house named Fallingwater because it was built over a waterfall, and the Imperial Hotel in Tokyo.

 Diplomacy and International Relations

From the beginning, the U.S. Government followed an "isolationist" policy. They were aloof from the happenings around them. However, World War I brought the country into the fray for a brief period and established the United States as a powerful nation. It is this isolationist policy that led the United States to refrain from joining the League of Nations following World War I.

The U.S. has to defend its many international bases. It has to defend its allies and friends in case of aggression from other countries. Now, being the only Superpower of the world, it has many other tasks to perform. There are countries under military pact with the U.S. There are threats to free will as well as democracy. There is the scourge of dictatorship in certain countries which threatens to undermine people's right to self-determination. And, after 9/11, the dreaded threat to free nations through fanatical terrorism has become real!

There are one billion people throughout the world living in abject poverty. About ten million people die of malnutrition and diseases arising out of malnutrition – almost 50% of which are children, mostly from developing or least developed nations. And the fact is that the U.S. is selling goods to the very same countries, which works out to much more than what it sells to the whole of West and Eastern Europe! The U.S. in fact has a responsibility towards such poor nations.

On the one hand, the U.S. has to support its friends, allies and countries on defense pacts, and on the other, to aid and comfort the poor nations by bilateral or multilateral channeling of funds. The Cuban crisis showed the U.S. could make a tough diplomatic decision. The wars in Korea and Vietnam were a diplomatic way of halting the scourge of communism spreading to other parts of Asia and elsewhere. The war in Afghanistan was waged to annihilate terrorism. The war in Iraq was aimed to unseat a dictator who steadfastly undermined the right of the people to self-determination. The innumerable instances of help to developing and least developed countries are again a diplomatic way of mitigating poverty.

Critics all over the world will always say that the U.S. has no authority to intervene in the lives of poor nations. A country which is the only reigning Superpower has the responsibility to help weaker countries to come up. The United States is doing this most diplomatically.

Sample Test Questions

1) From what country, during the New Immigration period of 1865-1910, did the majority of immigrants originate?

   A) Northern Europe
   B) Southeast Asia
   C) Southern and Eastern Europe
   D) Eastern Europe and Northern Asia
   E) Western and Central Europe

The correct answer is C:) Southern and Eastern Europe. The people were fleeing from poverty in their own nations.

2) Who was responsible for the "New Deal"?

   A) Franklin D Roosevelt
   B) Richard Nixon
   C) Ronald Reagan
   D) George Bush
   E) Jimmy Carter

The correct answer is A:) Franklin D Roosevelt.

3) Which amendment ensured voting rights for all citizens, regardless of race?

   A) 12th Amendment
   B) 13th Amendment
   C) 14th Amendment
   D) 15th Amendment
   E) 16th Amendment

The correct answer is D:) 15th Amendment. The 15th Amendment was passed in 1869, although extensive Jim Crow Laws and discriminatory practices in the South still stopped many blacks from voting.

4) Alice Paul is famous for her work in what?

   A) Women's Party
   B) NAACP
   C) Harlem Renaissance
   D) Jazz
   E) NRA

The correct answer is A:) Women's Party. Alice Paul was a feminist activist who worked for equal rights for women as leader of the National Women's Party.

5) Which civil rights leader advocated a theory of nonviolent direct action?

   A) Malcolm X
   B) Martin Luther King Jr.
   C) W. E. B. Dubois
   D) Booker T Washington
   E) Thurgood Marshall

The correct answer is B:) Martin Luther King Jr.

6) What were the major causes that lead to the Civil War?

   A) Eleven southern slave states declared their secession and intent for the expansion of slavery
   B) Election of Abraham Lincoln
   C) Political differences between the North and the South
   D) Formation of the Confederate States of America
   E) None of the above

The correct answer is A:) Eleven southern slave states declared their secession and intent for the expansion of slavery. Although there were many issues that helped to initiate the Civil War, the main issue that caused the Civil War was the eleven Southern Slave states declaring their secession and intent for the expansion of slavery.

7) Which of the following was NOT a belief of the Populist movement?

   A) Government aid for farmers
   B) Regulation of railroads
   C) National income tax
   D) Government support of trusts
   E) Favoring coinage of silver and paper money

The correct answer is D:) Government support of trusts. Trust was another name for monopoly. The Populist movement favored regulations of trusts such as the railroad industry.

8) What was the outcome of the Mexican American War, and the effects it had on the United States of America?

   A) Upon the victory of the Mexican American War, America gained half of the Mexican territory.
   B) The aftermath of the Mexican-American War was favorable to America as it gave them command and the region of Texas joining the American Union.
   C) The Mexican-American War gained the region of California and the respect of the nation.
   D) Upon the beneficial win of the Mexican-American War, America gained three-fourths of the Mexican territory.
   E) The aftermath of the Mexican-American War was favorable to the American people who gained the lands of New Mexico, Nevada and California.

The correct answer is A:) Upon the victory of the Mexican American War, America gained half of the Mexican territory.

9) In the Quarantine Speech, FDR spoke out against

   A) Communism
   B) WWII
   C) Red Scare
   D) Fascism
   E) None of the above

The correct answer is D:) Fascism.

10) What country did the majority of the immigrants that settled in the United States come from during the early 1800's?

A) Mexico
B) Europe
C) Ireland
D) France
E) None of the above

The correct answer is C:) Ireland. Due to the potato famine in Ireland, the majority of immigrants were of Irish descent.

11) The "Corrupt Bargain" resulted in

A) The election of Rutherford B Hayes as president
B) The spread and popularity of Jim Crow Laws
C) The Crime of 1873
D) A removal of Union troops from the South, ending Reconstruction
E) Both A and D

The correct answer is E:) Both A and D. The Corrupt Bargain, or Compromise of 1877 allowed Rutherford B Hayes to be pronounced President after a disputed election based on the unwritten deal that he would move troops out of the South, effectively ending Reconstruction.

12) Gone With the Wind was NOT

A) The recipient of a Pulitzer Prize
B) On the bestseller list multiple years in a row
C) Adapted to a film version
D) Printed more than 30 million times since it was published
E) None of the above

The correct answer is B:) On the bestseller list multiple years in a row.

13) Which of the following restricted the rights of Unions to strike?

   A) Wagner Act
   B) Taft-Hartley Act
   C) Social Security Act
   D) Sherman Act
   E) GI Bill

The correct answer is B:) Taft-Hartley Act. Enacted in 1947, the Taft-Hartley Act restricted the rights of Unions to strike and placed more regulations on union operations.

14) Tenements were

   A) Laws passed in the south after the Civil War which promoted segregation and racism.
   B) Upscale neighborhoods which developed in highly urban cities.
   C) Regulations which attempted to control the development of monopolies.
   D) Poorly constructed and overcrowded housing for poor urban workers.
   E) Early suburbs which allowed open space for people who commuted to cities for work.

The correct answer is D:) Poorly constructed and overcrowded housing for poor urban workers. Rapid urbanization caused a lack of good public health programs and a shortage of housing.

15) Which of the following provided veterans with job training and education assistance?

   A) Wagner Act
   B) Taft-Hartley Act
   C) Social Security Act
   D) Sherman Act
   E) GI Bill

The correct answer is E:) GI Bill.

16) Which of the following wrote The Sea Around Us?

    A) Rachel Carson
    B) Sylvia Plath
    C) Pearl Buck
    D) P.G. Wodehouse
    E) Fennimore Cooper

The correct answer is A:) Rachel Carson. Rachel Carson was a marine biologist who wrote the book Silent Spring and The Sea Around Us which significantly impacted and furthered the environmental movement.

17) During which of the following did the Palmer Raids occurred?

    A) Revolutionary War
    B) Korean War
    C) Red Scare
    D) Reconstruction
    E) None of the above

The correct answer is C:) Red Scare. When the Communist Party began gaining strength in the United States, it caused a panic resulting in the Palmer Raids. Thousands of suspected communists were jailed or deported.

18) What was one of the first methods of abolitionists?

    A) Print anti-slavery literature
    B) Put together conventions and lectures about anti-slavery
    C) Gather like-minded individuals together
    D) Arrange marches and anti-slavery demonstrations
    E) None of the above

The correct answer is C:) Gather like-minded individuals together. The first method of the abolitionists was to gather like-minded people together, other methods included publishing anti-slavery literature, holding lectures and organizing safety nets for freed slaves.

19) Which of the following most directly prompted United States involvement in WWII?

   A) Economic stake in the outcome
   B) Cuban Missile Crisis
   C) Atlanta Compromise
   D) Pearl Harbor
   E) Zimmerman Telegram

The correct answer is D:) Pearl Harbor. This was an attack on a United States Pacific Fleet in which 18 ships and 200 aircraft were destroyed, killing 3000 people. War was declared on Japan shortly after.

20) Austria-Hungary, Germany, and the Ottoman Empire were disintegrated due to what major American event?

   A) World War I
   B) The War of 1812
   C) World War II
   D) The War of Independence
   E) The Compromise of 1850

The correct answer is A:) World War I. World War I eventually disintegrated the Empires of the Austria-Hungary, Germany, and Ottoman.

21) Which president was known as a "trustbuster"?

   A) Grover Cleveland
   B) Theodore Roosevelt
   C) Woodrow Wilson
   D) Franklin D Roosevelt
   E) Herbert Hoover

The correct answer is B:) Theodore Roosevelt. His actions toward the end of trusts and many cases brought against trusts under the Sherman Antitrust Act earned him this nickname.

22) Which of the following wrote The Spy?

   A) Rachel Carson
   B) Sylvia Plath
   C) Pearl Buck
   D) P.G. Wodehouse
   E) Fennimore Cooper

The correct answer is E:) Fennimore Cooper.

23) Who wrote The Feminine Mystique?

   A) Betty Friedan
   B) Rosa Parks
   C) Alice Paul
   D) Betty Davis
   E) Susan B. Anthony

The correct answer is A:) Betty Friedan.

24) Robert LaFollete was a leader of which movement?

   A) Populism
   B) Radical Republicanism
   C) Social Gospel Movement
   D) Social Darwinism
   E) Progressivism

The correct answer is E:) Progressivism.

25) What was the major effect of Uncle Tom's Cabin on society?

   A) It produced sympathy and understanding for the horrible treatment of slaves.
   B) It was said to have been the main source for abolition movements and was thought to have laid the groundwork for the American Civil War.
   C) It reached out to Northerners who eventually became members of Anti-slavery movements.
   D) Made Southern Slaveholders to be nicer to their slaves.
   E) None of the above

The correct answer is B:) It was said to have been the main source for abolition movements and was thought to have laid the groundwork for the American Civil War. When the author met with Abraham Lincoln he was said to have commented, "So, this is the little lady who made this big war."

26) Which of the following made the purposeful creation of monopolies illegal?

   A) Roosevelt Corollary
   B) Truman Doctrine
   C) Sherman Antitrust Act
   D) 18th Amendment
   E) 17th Amendment

The correct answer is C:) Sherman Antitrust Act. The act essentially made purposely creating a monopoly illegal in an attempt to control the development of monopolies harmful to the economy.

27) Although many different aspects, combined with time and incidents, caused World War I, many individuals had plenty of their own opinions. Who was the President during that time and what was his opinion of the causes of the World War I?

   A) President Woodrow Wilson. He and others blamed the war on the assassination of Archduke Franz Ferdinand, the heir to the Austro-Hungarian throne.
   B) President William Howard Taft. He blamed the war on militarist ideology, which is the doctrinal view of society being best served when people of the militaries concepts govern it.
   C) President William Howard Taft. He blamed the war on the assassination of Archduke Franz Ferdinand, the heir to the Austro-Hungarian throne.
   D) President Warren G. Harding. He blamed the war on the militarist ideology, which is the doctrinal view of society being best served when people of the militaries concepts govern it.
   E) President Woodrow Wilson. He blamed the war on the militarist ideology, which is the doctrinal view of society being best served when people of the military's concepts govern it.

The correct answer is E:) President Woodrow Wilson. He blamed the war on the militarist ideology, which is the doctrinal view of society being best served when people of the military's concepts govern it.

28) Eugene V. Debs was known for:

   A) His participation in the Chicago Pullman Palace Car Company strike
   B) His position in the American Railway Union
   C) His position in the Socialist party
   D) None of the above
   E) All of the above

The correct answer is E:) All of the above.

29) Rosie the Riveter was NOT

   A) A fictional character portrayed as the ideal woman worker: loyal, efficient, patriotic, and pretty.
   B) An important part of the women's suffrage movement.
   C) A widely publicized image and song.
   D) Part of a government propaganda campaign to enlist women into the workforce.
   E) None of the above

The correct answer is B:) An important part of the women's suffrage movement.

30) Which of the following people founded the NAACP?

   A) W. E. B. Dubois
   B) Booker T Washington
   C) Martin Luther King Jr.
   D) Malcolm X
   E) None of the above

The correct answer is A:) W. E. B. Dubois. Dubois was a civil rights activist who favored more militant policies.

31) The right to form unions and use collective bargaining was a result of which of the following?

   A) Wagner Act
   B) Taft-Hartley Act
   C) Social Security Act
   D) Sherman Act
   E) GI Bill

The correct answer is A:) Wagner Act. Enacted in 1935, the Wagner Act, also called The National Labor Relations Act, resulted in the creation of the permanent National Labor Relations Board.

32) Which of the following was NOT included in President Wilson's Fourteen Points?

   I. Freedom of the Seas
   II. League of Nations
   III. Reduction of Arms

   A) II only
   B) II and III only
   C) I and II only
   D) I and III only
   E) I, II and III

The correct answer is E:) I, II and III. The Fourteen Points were Wilson's contribution to the Versailles treaty ending WWI.

33) The _____ prevents companies from creating monopolies in certain industries.

   A) Wagner Act
   B) Taft-Hartley Act
   C) Social Security Act
   D) Sherman Act
   E) GI Bill

The correct answer is D:) Sherman Act. The Sherman Act is also called the Sherman Anti-trust Act. Passed in 1890, it prohibits monopolies or combinations of businesses that discourage competition.

34) Which of the following encouraged westward migration?

   A) Homestead Act
   B) Compromise of 1877
   C) Cuban Missile Crisis
   D) Sherman Antitrust Act
   E) Roosevelt Corollary

The correct answer is A:) Homestead Act. It offered free land to people who agreed to move and settle the West.

35) What was the basic meaning behind the Emancipation Proclamation?

   A) The Emancipation Proclamation was a congressional order to free all the slaves in the United States of America.
   B) The Proclamation simply stated that all slaves in the Union states be free and have the same rights and privileges as all other citizens in the North.
   C) The Emancipation Proclamation was a presidential order to free all slaves in the area of the Confederate States of America.
   D) The proclamation stated that all free slaves within the Union and the Confederate states should be enacted into the United States as normal abiding citizens.
   E) None of the above

The correct answer is C:) The Emancipation Proclamation was a presidential order to free all slaves in the area of the Confederate States of America.

36) Which person wrote The Bell Jar?

   A) Dylan Thomas
   B) Robert Hayden
   C) Robert Frost
   D) Sylvia Plath
   E) Henry David Thoreau

The correct answer is D:) Sylvia Plath.

37) Who was the first black Supreme Court Justice?

   A) Booker T Washington
   B) Thurgood Marshall
   C) Martin Luther King Jr.
   D) Dred Scott
   E) None of the above

The correct answer is B:) Thurgood Marshall. Marshall was also the head lawyer in the case of Brown v. Board of Education.

38) When Conscription was passed, what were the fears of those who opposed it?

   A) Soldiers who were forced into battle would make poor fighting men and it compromised volunteer soldiers from enlisting, seeing the conscription as an act of desperation.
   B) That conscription would cause riots led by rioters who opposed the war and were not willing to fight for it.
   C) Those who opposed the conscription felt it was an invasion of individual interests and feared those who were forced to fight would give up easily and help their opponents win the battle, or surrender to end the war.
   D) Conscription would make volunteer soldiers have low mortality rates; by the thought of the desperation of war hands, their spirits would be broken.
   E) None of the above

The correct answer is A:) Soldiers who were forced into battle would make poor fighting men and it compromised volunteer soldiers from enlisting, seeing the conscription as an act of desperation.

39) "Double V" referred to a "double victory" over what two issues?

   A) WWII and racism
   B) WWI and racism
   C) WWII and women's rights
   D) WWI and women's rights
   E) All of the above

The correct answer is A:) WWII and racism.

40) Alger Hiss was convicted and sentenced to prison for what?

   A) Espionage
   B) Treason
   C) Perjury
   D) None of the above
   E) All of the above

The correct answer is C:) Perjury. Though suspected and accused of espionage, he was never convicted.

41) In which case did the Supreme Court establish that segregation in public schools was unconstitutional?

   A) Brown v. Board of Education
   B) Roe v. Wade
   C) Plessy v. Ferguson
   D) MuCulloch v. Maryland
   E) Baker v. Carr

The correct answer is A:) Brown v. Board of Education. This overturned the case of Plessy v. Ferguson which allowed "separate but equal" schools.

42) Who said "what you farmers need to do is raise less corn and more Hell"?

   A) Mary Elizabeth Clyens
   B) Rosa Parks
   C) Alice Paul
   D) Betty Davis
   E) Susan B. Anthony

The correct answer is A:) Mary Elizabeth Clyens. A member of the Populist Party, she was a political supporter of woman's suffrage, prohibition, and birth control.

43) Which of the following allowed for the direct election of Senators by the people?

   A) Constitution
   B) Bill of Rights
   C) 17th Amendment
   D) Civil Rights Act
   E) 15th Amendment

The correct answer is C:) 17th Amendment. The 17th Amendment was passed in 1912. It modified the Constitution to allow people to elect Senators, where originally they had been chosen by state legislatures.

44) Who wrote On the Road?

   A) William S. Burroughs
   B) Jack Kerouac
   C) Allen Ginsberg
   D) William Whyte
   E) None of the above

The correct answer is B:) Jack Kerouac. He was known as part of a literary consortium known as the "Beats" which rejected the typical mainstream culture as well as promoting experimentation with illegal drugs and sexuality. Other famous "beatnik" works include Allen Ginsberg's Howl (1956), and William S. Burroughs's Naked Lunch (1959).

45) "Trust yourself. You know more than you think you do," are the famous words in what book?

   A) Gone with the Wind
   B) Common Sense Book of Baby and Child Care
   C) Catcher in the Rye
   D) Rebel without a Cause
   E) Death of a Salesman

The correct answer is B:) Common Sense Book of Baby and Child Care.

46) In the 1908 Muller v. Oregon case, Muller violates an Oregon state law restricting what?

   A) Minimum wage for women in factories
   B) Maximum wage for women in factories
   C) Minimum work hours for women in factories
   D) Maximum work hours for women in factories
   E) None of the above

The correct answer is D:) Maximum work hours for women in factories.

47) Which of the following best describes the agreement which ended the Cuban Missile Crisis?

   A) The Soviet Union dismantled the launch sites and the United States agreed to not invade Cuba.
   B) The United States agreed to allow the Soviet Union to build the launch sites as long as they could build their own in Turkey.
   C) The Soviet Union refused to dismantle the launch sites and the United States eventually backed down because they couldn't do anything about it.
   D) The Soviet Union agreed to dismantle the launch sites and apologized for making the United States nervous.
   E) The Soviet Union agreed to dismantle the launch sites as long as the United States dismantled their own launch sites in Turkey.

The correct answer is A:) The Soviet Union dismantled the launch sites and the United States agreed to not invade Cuba.

48) Who was the founder of the American Birth Control League?

   A) Mary Elizabeth Clyens
   B) Rosa Parks
   C) Alice Paul
   D) Betty Davis
   E) Margaret Higgins Sanger Slee

The correct answer is E:) Margaret Higgins Sanger Slee. She was the founder of the American Birth Control League which later became Planned Parenthood.

49) Who said "I will fight no more forever"?

   A) Geronimo
   B) Chief Joseph
   C) Tuekakas
   D) Sitting Bull
   E) None of the above

The correct answer is B:) Chief Joseph. He was a leader of a band of Nez Perce Native Americans who were forcibly relocated by the United States government.

50) What was the name given to the group who believed that Lincoln had been too kind, and favored punishment of the South after the Civil War?

   A) Mugwumps
   B) Extremist Democrats
   C) Extremist Republicans
   D) Radical Democrats
   E) Radical Republicans

The correct answer is E:) Radical Republicans.

51) Which of the following was a famous journalist and photographer?

   A) Mary Elizabeth Clyens
   B) Jack Kerouac
   C) Michael Harrington
   D) Jacob Riis
   E) None of the above

The correct answer is D:) Jacob Riis. Riis was famous for his photographic and journalistic efforts in New York City. He helped develop tenements in the city. These are sometimes referred to as "dumbbell" tenements because the shape of the floor-plan resembles a dumbbell. The design was important to let not only light into the apartments but fresh air via a ventilation shaft as well. His famous work was entitled How the Other Half Lives.

52) Which of the following wrote The Good Earth?

   A) Rachel Carson
   B) Sylvia Plath
   C) Pearl Buck
   D) P.G. Wodehouse
   E) Fennimore Cooper

The correct answer is C:) Pearl Buck. Pearl S. Buck's book The Good Earth won her the Nobel Prize.

53) A movement towards charity and social responsibility in the late 1800s was called the

   A) Square Deal philosophy
   B) Social Gospel movement
   C) Public Programs initiative
   D) Second Great Awakening
   E) None of the above

The correct answer is B:) Social Gospel movement. The movement continued into the early 1900s. The Second Great Awakening was a religious movement, and the Square Deal was Roosevelt's term for his intention to protect the rights of the working class.

54) If you were a member of this group in the mid-1900's, you would have goals that included preventing war through collective security, attempting to settle disputes between countries by negotiations, and to improve a more global welfare of humanity. Which group would you have been a member of?

   A) The Ku Klux Klan, organized in the 1920's
   B) The League of Nations formed in 1919
   C) The U.S. Securities Commission established in 1934
   D) The National Industrial Recovery Act, founded in 1933
   E) The Federal Emergency Relief Administration, created in 1932

The correct answer is B:) The League of Nations, formed in 1919. The League of Nations was founded as a result of the Paris Peace Conference in 1919.

55) The 14th Amendment

   A) Allows Congress to levy income taxes.
   B) Defined the term end date for the President, Vice President, and representatives in Congress.
   C) Gave women the right to vote.
   D) Officially ended slavery in the United States.
   E) Ensured due process and equal protection under the law, defined citizenship and declared that the U.S. government would not pay compensation for freed slaves.

The correct answer is E:) Ensured due process and equal protection under the law, defined citizenship and declared that the U.S. government would not pay compensation for freed slaves. The 14th Amendment was passed in 1866.

56) What was the controversy over the conviction of Nicola Sacco and Bartolomeo Venzetti?

   A) Sacco and Venzetti did not receive a fair trial
   B) Boda should have been arrested, not Sacco and Venzetti
   C) The murder weapon did not belong to Sacco or Venzetti
   D) Sacco and Venzetti acted in self-defense
   E) None of the above

The correct answer is A:) Sacco and Venzetti did not receive a fair trial.

57) Which is NOT true of the 1911 Triangle Shirtwaist fire?

   A) One hundred forty-six people died
   B) Blanck and Harris were found guilty of manslaughter
   C) The elevators, fire escape, and fire hoses all failed to be very helpful
   D) The fire was put out in thirty minutes
   E) None of the above

The correct answer is B:) Blanck and Harris were found guilty of manslaughter.

58) *The Birth of a Nation* was the title of

   A) A book
   B) A play
   C) A movie
   D) A movement
   E) A journal

The correct answer is C:) A movie. This movie was originally entitled *The Clansman* which was based on a book and play by Thomas Dixon with the same name. This silent movie came out in 1915 and was highly controversial due to the fact it portrayed the Ku Klux Klan positively and heroically.

59) New Federalism was

   A) Nixon's slogan for returning power and resources to states and people.
   B) Roosevelt's philosophy that a strong national government should protect the underprivileged and promote social justice.
   C) A movement of the late 1800s to early 1900s which emphasized social responsibility and charity.
   D) President Truman's policy stating that the United States would offer financial and military support to countries to stop the spread of Communism.
   E) Wilson's contribution to the Versailles treaty ending WWI, including freedom of the seas and the League of Nations.

The correct answer is A:) Nixon's slogan for returning power and resources to states and people.

60) Which of the following Supreme Court cases dealt with the topic of jurors being excluded from hearing a case based on race?

   A) Dred Scott v. Sanford
   B) Norris v. Alabama
   C) Plessy v. Ferguson
   D) Marbury v. Madison
   E) Schenck v. United States

The correct answer is B:) Norris v. Alabama. This very famous case was also known as Scottsboro Boys or Scottsboro Nine. The case dealt with nine young homeless black defendants accused of raping two homeless white women. The juries that heard their cases were entirely white, their counsel unprepared and eight of the nine were sentenced to death. The case was appealed twice before the Supreme Court.

61) What Amendment protected Johnson's actions in the 1989 Texas v. Johnson case?

   A) The First Amendment
   B) The Fifth Amendment
   C) The Thirteenth Amendment
   D) The Fourteenth Amendment
   E) The Eighteenth Amendment

The correct answer is A:) The First Amendment. Johnson's actions were determined to be symbolic speech protected under the First Amendment.

62) In what year was the Boy Scouts of America organization was founded?

   A) 1900
   B) 1910
   C) 1920
   D) 1930
   E) 1943

The correct answer is B:) 1910.

63) In which Japanese city was the first atomic bomb detonated in WWII?

   A) Nagasaki
   B) Tokyo
   C) Kyoto
   D) Honshu
   E) Hiroshima

The correct answer is E:) Hiroshima. The second bomb was dropped in Nagasaki a few days later.

64) Northerners who moved to the South with freedmen were known as what?

   A) Scalawags
   B) Carpetbaggers
   C) Scabs
   D) Sharecroppers
   E) None of the above

The correct answer is B:) Carpetbaggers. Carpetbaggers were Northerners who moved to the South with freedmen. The phrase was originally coined from the term carpet bags, which are inexpensive luggage. Scalawags is a person who was White from the South who joined the Republican Party in the ex-Confederate area during reconstruction.

65) As Communism began to spread after WWII, a plan was constructed providing for large scale economic aid to European countries to stop them from becoming communist. The plan was called

A) The Marshall Plan
B) The Truman Doctrine
C) The New Deal
D) The Roosevelt Corollary
E) The Homestead Act

The correct answer is A:) The Marshall Plan. It was developed by Truman's Secretary of State, George C Marshall. It was also called the European Recovery Program.

66) The Civil Rights Act of 1964 was a piece of landmark legislature that was indicted into law on July 2, 1964. What were the major implications of the Civil Rights Act?

A) It protested against the discrimination of individuals based on their race, color, or national origin in voting and employment only.
B) It outlawed discrimination based on race, color, religion, sex, or national origin in voting, employment, and all public services, including transportation and public schooling.
C) It outlawed discrimination based on sex in voting, employment, and public services, including transportation and public schooling.
D) It outlawed discrimination based on race, color, religion, sex, or national origin in voting, employment, and public services, excluding transportation and public schooling.
E) It protested against the discrimination of individuals based on their race, color, sex, or national origin in employment and public services only.

The correct answer is B:) It outlawed discrimination based on race, color, religion, sex, or national origin in voting, employment, and all public services, including transportation and public schooling.

67) President Theodore Roosevelt's philosophy that a strong national government was responsible for protecting citizens and promoting social justice is called

   A) New Nationalism
   B) New Federalism
   C) New Deal
   D) Square Deal
   E) Social Gospel Movement

The correct answer is A:) New Nationalism.

68) Who wrote Moby Dick?

   A) Edgar Allen Poe
   B) Washington Irving
   C) Herman Melville
   D) Pearl S. Buck
   E) Samuel Langhorne Clemens

The correct answer is C:) Herman Melville.

69) Which of the following was the creator of fictional character Jeeves?

   A) Rachel Carson
   B) Sylvia Plath
   C) Pearl Buck
   D) P.G. Wodehouse
   E) Fennimore Cooper

The correct answer is D:) P.G. Wodehouse.

70) Who was the first person to run under the American Independent Party?

   A) George C Marshall
   B) Zachary Taylor
   C) Booker T Washington
   D) George Wallace
   E) Rutherford B Hayes

The correct answer is D:) George Wallace. He ran in 1968 and was popular in the South and among blue collar workers.

71) What is the name of the movie that symbolizes the Cold War through a teenager's fight with a bully?

   A) *Rebel Without a Cause*
   B) *Catcher in the Rye*
   C) *Gone with the Wind*
   D) *American Gothic*
   E) *The Wild West*

The correct answer is A:) *Rebel Without a Cause*.

72) Who wrote The Adventures of Huckleberry Finn?

   A) Edgar Allen Poe
   B) P.G. Wodehouse
   C) Herman Melville
   D) Pearl S. Buck
   E) Mark Twain

The correct answer is E:) Mark Twain.

73) Which amendment gave women the right to vote, and in what year was it passed?

   A) 18th Amendment, 1917
   B) 19th Amendment, 1919
   C) 20th Amendment, 1920
   D) 19th Amendment, 1932
   E) 20th Amendment, 1919

The correct answer is B:) 19th Amendment, 1919. The 18th Amendment made the manufacture and sale of alcohol illegal and the 20th Amendment defined term end dates for the President, Vice President and Congress.

74) If you are a part of a union that "defends and preserves the individual rights and liberties of every person in the United States of America by its own constitution and laws governing it," you are most likely in the…

   A) Union Network International
   B) American Defense Union
   C) American Civil Liberties Union
   D) The Universal Defense Union
   E) International Union

The correct answer is C:) The American Civil Liberties Union.

75) How many suspected communists were jailed or deported as a result of the Palmer Raids?

   A) 100
   B) 450
   C) 1,000
   D) 4,000
   E) 60,000

The correct answer is D:) 4,000. When the Communist Party began gaining strength in the United States it caused a panic resulting in the Palmer Raids. Over 4,000 suspected (unverified) communists were jailed or deported.

76) Who wrote The Fall of the House of Usher?

   A) Edgar Allen Poe
   B) P.G. Wodehouse
   C) Herman Melville
   D) Pearl S. Buck
   E) Samuel Langhorne Clemens

The correct answer is A:) Edgar Allen Poe.

77) Northern Securities was dismantled under the Sherman Anti-Trust Act because

   A) As a monopoly, it restrained free trade
   B) The federal government had controlling interest of railroad companies
   C) They obtained the property illegally
   D) Their permits were not up to date
   E) None of the above

The correct answer is A:) As a monopoly, it restrained free trade.

78) *American Gothic* was painted by

   A) Alger Hiss
   B) John Rockefeller
   C) Grant Wood
   D) Benjamin Spock
   E) Picasso

The correct answer is C:) Grant Wood.

79) The Truman Doctrine showed that President Truman wanted to stop the spread of

   A) Fascism
   B) Disease
   C) Communism
   D) Poverty
   E) Both B and D

The correct answer is C:) Communism. The policy stated that the United States would offer financial and military support to countries in an effort to stop the spread of communism.

80) The _____ theory is based on the principle that if one country has communist leadership, those countries around them will have undue influence and become communist countries also.

   A) Apple
   B) Leaf
   C) Tree
   D) Domino
   E) Snowball

The correct answer is D:) Domino.

81) The Ku Klux Klan was

   A) A group which specifically worked to stop the integration of public schools in the South.
   B) A foundation which advocated the free exercise of civil rights.
   C) A legally organized group which opposed black's rights.
   D) A white supremacist group formed after the Civil War which terrorized blacks.
   E) None of the above

The correct answer is D:) A white supremacist group formed after the Civil War which terrorized blacks. It was disbanded in 1869 but resurfaced in the early 1900s.

82) President John F. Kennedy's stay in office was noted with his famous speech, "Ask not what your country can do for you, but what you can do for your country." How many days, altogether, did President Kennedy serve as the President of the United States before his assassination?

   A) 1,000 days
   B) 1,500 days
   C) 900 days
   D) 1,200 days
   E) 950 days

The correct answer is A:) 1,000 days. President John F. Kennedy only served 1,000 days in office before he was assassinated in 1963.

83) The Coinage Law of 1873 was nicknamed what by its critics?

   A) The Crime of 1873
   B) Silver Act
   C) Compromise of 1873
   D) Gold Standard Law
   E) None of the above

The correct answer is A:) The Crime of 1873. The law removed silver from circulation as money.

84) Who wrote Unsafe at Any Speed?

   A) Mary Elizabeth Clyens
   B) Jack Kerouac
   C) Michael Harrington
   D) Ralph Nader
   E) Upton Sinclair

The correct answer is D:) Ralph Nader.

85) Which photographer was well known for their work in the Depression?

   A) William de Kooning
   B) Jasper Johns
   C) Claes Oldenburg
   D) Dorothea Lange
   E) Ann Hamilton

The correct answer is D:) Dorothea Lange. In addition to being a talented photographer, she was married to the famous painter Maynard Dixon.

86) The Haymarket Affair was

   A) An attempt to control the development of monopolies harmful to the economy.
   B) A speech in which FDR spoke out against fascism and compared it to a contagious disease that should be quarantined.
   C) An attack on a United States Pacific Fleet in which 18 ships and 200 aircraft were destroyed, along with 3000 people killed.
   D) Also known as the "Corrupt Bargain," this compromise allowed Rutherford B Hayes to be pronounced President after a disputed election based on the unwritten deal that he would move troops out of the South.
   E) A workers riot in Chicago in which a number of police and citizens died.

The correct answer is E:) A workers riot in Chicago in which a number of police and citizens died. Because the participants were mainly minority races, it sparked controversy and hatred.

87) Who wrote <u>Rip Van Winkle</u>?

A) Edgar Allen Poe
B) P.G. Wodehouse
C) Herman Melville
D) Pearl Buck
E) Washington Irving

The correct answer is E:) Washington Irving.

88) FDR's plan to bring economic relief to the country during the Great Depression was called:

A) New Federalism
B) New Nationalism
C) New Deal
D) Federal Aid Program
E) None of the above

The correct answer is C:) New Deal. During his presidency many new government programs were created to increase the standard of living and create jobs, including the CCC, CWA, FERA, FHA, AAA, SEC and FDIC.

89) The 1920 census collected which of the following

A) Name
B) Race
C) Age
D) Literacy
E) All of the above

The correct answer is E:) All of the above. The census also collected information about the birth place and language spoken. What makes 1920 significant is that it is the first year the date for the census was moved to January 1st by the request of the Department of Agriculture to be more accurate in counting livestock and farmhands.

90) Which of the following, passed at the end of the Civil War, officially ended slavery in the United States?

   A) Emancipation Proclamation
   B) 12th Amendment
   C) 13th Amendment
   D) 14th Amendment
   E) Civil Rights Act

The correct answer is C:) 13th Amendment. The Emancipation Proclamation freed all slaves in areas of rebellion (the South), but slavery wasn't officially abolished until 1865 when the 13th Amendment was passed.

91) Which of the following wrote The History of the Standard Oil Company?

   A) Dorothea Lange
   B) Pearl Buck
   C) Ida Tarbell
   D) P.G. Wodehouse
   E) None of the above

The correct answer is C:) Ida Tarbell. Her book, written in 1904, has been recognized by one of the top 100 works of American journalism this century.

92) Which of the following best describes the Monroe Doctrine?

   A) Began a large scale economic project which involved strengthening economic foundations in European countries as a method of combating the spread of Communism.
   B) Stated that the United States would intervene to maintain stability in South American countries.
   C) Stated that the United States would offer financial and military support to countries in an effort to stop the spread of Communism.
   D) A statement which forbid further colonization of the Western hemisphere by European countries.
   E) All of the above are correct

The correct answer is D:) A statement which forbid further colonization of the Western hemisphere by European countries. Answer A describes the Marshal Plan, answer B describes the Roosevelt Corollary and C describes the Truman Doctrine.

93) A political idea that compares the goals, wishes and rights of the normal man to those of the "elites" is known as

   A) Progressivism
   B) Populism
   C) Suffrage
   D) Darwinism
   E) None of the above

The correct answer is B:) Populism.

94) What does SALT I stand for?

   A) Soviet Arms Limitation Talks I
   B) Strategic Arms Limitation Treaty I
   C) Soviet Arms Limitation Treaty I
   D) Strategic Arms Limitation Talks I
   E) None of the above

The correct answer is D:) Strategic Arms Limitation Talks I.

95) Which of the following was NOT an aim of progressivism?

   A) Remove corruption from government
   B) Government should create an even playing field in economics
   C) Church should play a role in social change
   D) Include all citizens in politics
   E) The government should play a role in social change

The correct answer is C:) Church should play a role in social change. Those who believe in progressivism thought that corruption needed to be removed from the government, that the government should create an even playing field in economics and social change. They also believed that all citizens should participate in the political process.

96) The 18th Amendment prohibited which of the following?

   A) The creation of laws limiting free speech
   B) The formation of monopolies
   C) The illegal search and seizure of property
   D) The manufacture and sale of alcohol
   E) None of the above

The correct answer is D:) The manufacture and sale of alcohol. The 18th Amendment was passed in 1917, and was later repealed.

97) Which of the following wrote <u>Tom Sawyer</u>?

   A) Edgar Allen Poe
   B) P.G. Wodehouse
   C) Herman Melville
   D) Pearl S. Buck
   E) Samuel Langhorne Clemens

The correct answer is E:) Samuel Langhorne Clemens. He wrote under the name Mark Twain.

98) Which of the following were NOT involved with the Scopes trial?

   A) John Scopes
   B) Clarence Darrow
   C) William Jennings Bryan
   D) Henry Washington Bates
   E) All of the above

The correct answer is D:) Henry Washington Bates. All of the other names were involved in the trial as the accused or the legal representation.

99) Emma Goldman was an advocate of

   A) Freedom of expression
   B) Equality and independence for women
   C) Radical education
   D) Union organization and worker's rights
   E) All of the above

The correct answer is E:) All of the above.

100) Which of the following BEST describes settlement houses?

A) A community living arrangement with a goal of social reform and improving the standard of living in low income areas.
B) Houses where immigrants were allowed to stay overnight upon entering the country.
C) Institutions that helped individuals in lawsuits that could not afford the payments that they were ordered to make.
D) Community houses for individuals who were leaving the prison system and seeking to change their lives.
E) Live-in boarding school systems for upper class individuals.

The correct answer is A:) A community living arrangement with a goal of social reform and improving the standard of living in low income areas. The houses were motivated particularly by women with a goal of social reform. The houses hosted many neighborhood programs such as Mothers' clubs, English learning classes, art groups, music groups, sports teams, and in some cases summer camps and school systems. They also became important political forces as well.

101) Which country did the United States NOT take control of as a result of the Spanish American War?

A) Guam
B) Philippines
C) Cuba
D) Puerto Rico
E) Venezuela

The correct answer is E:) Venezuela. The Spanish American War resulted in United States control of Puerto Rico, the Philippines, Guam and Cuba. The war ended Spanish involvement in the Americas.

102) Who was known as the "Father of Pan-Africanism"?

A) Martin Luther King Jr.
B) W.E.B. Du Bois
C) Booker T. Washington
D) Malcolm X
E) None of the above

The correct answer is B:) W.E.B. Du Bois. Pan-Africanism is a movement or philosophy designed to unify all those of African heritage.

103) When was Catcher in the Rye by J. D. Salinger first published?

   A) 1941
   B) 1951
   C) 1961
   D) 1971
   E) 1971

The correct answer is B:) 1951.

104) Who of the following was NOT one of the "Big Four" after WWI?

   A) Prime Minister David Lloyd George
   B) President Wilson
   C) Premier Georges Clemenceau
   D) Tsar Nicholas II
   E) Premier Vittorio Orlando

The correct answer is D:) Tsar Nicholas II. He was the leader of the Soviet Union. The Big Four were the leaders of the Britain, France, Italy and the United States (A, C, E and B respectively).

105) Who gave the speech "I Dreamed a Dream"?

   A) Martin Luther King Jr.
   B) W.E.B. Du Bois
   C) Booker T. Washington
   D) Malcolm X
   E) None of the above

The correct answer is A:) Martin Luther King Jr.

106) The 20th Amendment

   A) Allows Congress to levy income taxes.
   B) Defined the term end date for the President, Vice President, and representatives in Congress.
   C) Gave women the right to vote.
   D) Officially ended slavery in the United States.
   E) Ensured due process and equal protection under the law, defined citizenship and declared that the U.S. government would not pay compensation for freed slaves.

The correct answer is B:) Defined the term end date for the President, Vice President, and representatives in Congress. The 20th Amendment was passed in 1932.

107) Which of the following Acts allotted land to the American Indians?

   A) Emergency Immigration Act
   B) Neutrality Act
   C) Immigration Reform and Control Act
   D) Dawes Act
   E) None of the above

The correct answer is D:) Dawes Act.

108) Which of the following is NOT true of the Grandfather Clause?

   A) It was one type of Jim Crow Law in the post-Civil War South.
   B) It was widely popular throughout the entire country.
   C) It allowed a person to vote only if their grandfather could.
   D) It kept most blacks from voting, along with literacy tests and poll taxes.
   E) Both A and B are incorrect

The correct answer is B:) It was widely popular through the entire country. It was one of the Jim Crow Laws instituted in the South to keep blacks from voting.

109) Investigational journalists were also known as

   A) Separatists
   B) Muckrakers
   C) Code-talkers
   D) Fascism
   E) None of the above

The correct answer is B:) Muckrakers. Famous muckrakers include Ida Tarbell, Upton Sinclair and Jacob Riis.

110) The Harlem Renaissance was

   A) An attempt to control the development of monopolies harmful to the economy.
   B) A speech in which FDR spoke out against fascism and compared it to a contagious disease that should be quarantined.
   C) An attack on a United States Pacific Fleet in which 18 ships and 200 aircraft were destroyed, along with 3000 people killed.
   D) A literary movement headed by black writers in the 1920s and centered in New York.
   E) A workers riot in Chicago in which a number of police and citizens died.

The correct answer is D:) A literary movement headed by black writers in the 1920s and centered in New York. The Harlem Renaissance was also called the New Negro Movement.

111) Which of the following best describes the United States' response to the atrocities of the Hungarian uprising?

   A) Approval of the open and honest tactics of the Community party
   B) Immediate military intervention on behalf of the Hungarian people
   C) Criticism of the Hungarian people's failure to behave diplomatically
   D) Open opposition to Communist tactics, but failure to act
   E) None of the above

The correct answer is D:) Open opposition to Communist tactics, but failure to act. Due to the concurrent events of the Suez crisis, the world focus was on other parts of the world at the time, despite strong opposition to the tactics used.

112) The Zimmerman Telegram was

A) The first telegram ever sent in the United States and was received in the Oval Office.
B) The telegram sent to the White House announcing the attack on Pearl Harbor and prompting WWII.
C) A telegram from the leader of Germany announcing surrender in WWI.
D) A message sent from Germany to Mexico, requesting an alliance against the United States.
E) None of the above

The correct answer is D:) A message sent from Germany to Mexico, requesting an alliance against the United States. As the United States was not involved in WWI at the time, the telegram increased support for the war.

113) Which of the following was a major African-American artistic movement?

A) Suffrage
B) Harlem Renaissance
C) NAACP
D) Prohibition
E) Abolition

The correct answer is B:) Harlem Renaissance. While all of the answer choices have something to do with African-Americans, only the Harlem Renaissance was an artistic and cultural movement. The Harlem Renaissance consisted of many authors and artists who depicted the various differences, strengths and culture of black America.

114) Which of the following allowed for expansion of the Vietnam war?

A) Platt Amendment
B) Gulf of Tonkin Resolution
C) Vietnam Pact
D) Teller Amendment
E) Warsaw Pact

The correct answer is B:) Gulf of Tonkin Resolution. Following reports of U.S. destroyers stationed in the Gulf of Tonkin in Vietnam being attacked by North Vietnam forces, President Johnson took immediate action and proposed the Gulf of Tonkin Resolution which would give him power to expand military efforts in Vietnam in any way that he deemed necessary to establish peace in the area.

115) Peace talks were held at Camp David between which two nations?

   A) Cuba and Russia
   B) Egypt and Israel
   C) West and East Germany
   D) Pakistan and Jordan
   E) None of the above

The correct answer is B:) Egypt and Israel.

116) Which country was NOT part of the League of Nations?

   A) England
   B) France
   C) United States
   D) Egypt
   E) None of the above

The correct answer is C:) United States. The League of Nations was formed after the end of WWI in the hopes of mediating any future disputes among countries so that another world war did not occur. The United States (Woodrow Wilson) chose NOT to join although some countries like Germany wished to join and were denied admittance.

117) Phyllis Schlafly is known for her opposition to the

   A) Platt Amendment
   B) Gulf of Tonkin Resolution
   C) Equal Rights Amendment
   D) Civil Rights Act
   E) Teller Amendment

The correct answer is C:) Equal Rights Amendment. Phyllis organized rallies, baked bread for legislators, and appeared on television all in an effort to prevent the passage of the amendment. She argued that the amendment would destroy conservative family values and would strongly disadvantage full time homemakers. Due in large part to her efforts, the bill was never passed.

118) Which of the following resulted in higher literacy rates for Mexican Americans?

A) Suffrage
B) Harlem Renaissance
C) Chicano Renaissance
D) Prohibition
E) Abolition

The correct answer is C:) Chicano Renaissance. Tomás Rivera wrote <u>The Harvest</u> which helped inform many about the conditions of migrant farm workers. A great essayist, he was known as one of the key figures in the Chicano Renaissance which took place in the 1960s where the literacy of Mexican Americans rose dramatically while living and working conditions also improved.

119) Which of the following is NOT a reason that the United States entered WWI?

A) Zimmerman Telegram
B) German submarine warfare
C) Lusitania
D) Pearl Harbor
E) All of the above

The correct answer is D:) Pearl Harbor. Pearl Harbor prompted United States involvement in WWII, not WWI. However, the Zimmerman Telegram, sinking of the Lusitania and unrestricted German submarine warfare all increased support for WWI.

120) "Separate but equal" is the description of

A) NAACP
B) League of Women Voters
C) UNIA
D) Jim Crow laws
E) None of the above

The correct answer is D:) Jim Crow laws.

121) Who said "Ask not what your country can do for you. Ask what you can do for your country."?

   A) Abraham Lincoln
   B) John F. Kennedy
   C) James Monroe
   D) Booker T Washington
   E) Martin Luther King Jr.

The correct answer is B:) John F. Kennedy. This quote was part of his inaugural address in 1961.

122) Who is famous for the Atlanta Compromise?

   A) George Marshall
   B) George Wallace
   C) James Monroe
   D) Booker T Washington
   E) Martin Luther King Jr.

The correct answer is D:) Booker T Washington. The Atlanta Compromise is a speech by Booker T Washington in which he encouraged education as a method of social advancement.

123) Which of the following does NOT have to do with WWII?

   A) Victory gardens
   B) "Dollar-a-year men"
   C) "No-strike" pledge
   D) WAVES
   E) None of the above

The correct answer is E:) None of the above. ALL of the above have to do with WWII. Victory gardens were where individuals planted their own food for their support. "Dollar-a-year men" were businessmen who moved to Washington to work for free, without pay, on war agencies and production. Labor unions agreed on a "no-strike" pledge for the duration of the ware. WAVES stands for Women Accepted for Volunteer Emergency Service.

124) The 16th Amendment allowed Congress to

    A) Enforce due process for all citizens
    B) Create laws limiting free speech in times of war
    C) Levy income taxes
    D) Overrule the Supreme Court in extreme cases
    E) Declare war

The correct answer is C:) Levy income taxes. It was passed in 1909.

125) Who led the invasion of the Allied forces on D-Day?

    A) Eisenhower
    B) MacArthur
    C) Stalin
    D) Truman
    E) Roosevelt

The correct answer is A:) Eisenhower.

126) The Compromise of 1877 was also called the

    A) Corrupt Bargain
    B) Missouri Compromise
    C) Square Deal
    D) Crime of 1877
    E) Atlanta Compromise

The correct answer is A:) Corrupt Bargain. This compromise allowed Rutherford B Hayes to be pronounced President after a disputed election based on the unwritten deal that he would move troops out of the South, effectively ending Reconstruction.

127) Which of the following was NOT a cause of the Great Depression?

    A) Economic class inequality
    B) Poor banking regulations
    C) Not enough factory production
    D) Excess farm production
    E) None of the above

The correct answer is C:) Not enough factory production. Economic class inequality, poor banking regulations, excess farm production and excess factory production led to the conditions that caused the Great Depression.

128) Who wrote Death of a Salesman?

   A) Arthur Miller
   B) Jack Kerouac
   C) Michael Harrington
   D) Jacob Riis
   E) Upton Sinclair

The correct answer is A:) Arthur Miller.

129) The Teller Amendment was an attempt to

   A) Avoid further conflict in Cuba by withdrawing all American business from the country.
   B) Gain support for the Spanish American War by assuring the public that control of Cuba was not the government's main objective.
   C) Unite with Spain in squashing a rebellion that was forming in Cuba.
   D) Proclaim the United States' desire to ensure "pacification" of rebelling people in southern Spain, and their continued support for the Spanish government.
   E) State the United States' objective to colonize the island of Cuba once liberated from Spanish rule.

The correct answer is B:) Gain support for the Spanish American War by assuring the public that control of Cuba was not the government's main objective. The Teller Amendment was passed just five days before the official start of the Spanish American War. It stated that the United States had no intention to annex the island of Cuba, but was rather engaging in the Spanish American War in order to liberate the Cuban people from Spanish rule and give them their independence.

130) The film *Dr. Strangelove* is a commentary about which war?

   A) Cold War
   B) Vietnam War
   C) Korean War
   D) WWII
   E) Spanish American War

The correct answer is A:) Cold War. The film is a political satire centered on the question of nuclear war. The movie was released not long after the Cuban Missile Crisis and launch of Sputnik. It was a time of widespread worry about the possibility of nuclear war. The film depicts the events and decisions by government officials leading to such a war in a comical way.

131) Who was famed for their theories of a social elite composed of government, military, and corporate individuals that effectively destroyed true equality in America?

A) Frank Lloyd Wright
B) Karl Marx
C) Sigmund Freud
D) C. Wright Mills
E) Phyllis Schafly

The correct answer is D:) C. Wright Mills. In his book <u>The Power Elite</u>, Mills makes the argument that there is no such thing as true democracy in the United States. Rather, he argued that certain key people in government, military, and the corporate world held the majority of influence and authority that left the average citizen with little power.

132) In 1898 the Philippines were ceded to the United States by

A) Russia
B) France
C) Britain
D) Spain
E) Turkey

The correct answer is D:) Spain.

133) Which of the following BEST describes the Filipino Insurrection?

A) A minor conflict in which Spain asked for the help of U.S. military in creating a naval blockade.
B) A three-year fight for Filipino independence in which 4,000 American troops and 500,000 Filipino citizens died.
C) A series of short battles fought by the Philippines after they gained their independence in 1935.
D) A wide-scale revolt by the Philippines in which the U.S. asked for Spanish and French help in protecting American citizens in the country.
E) A battle in which the people of the Philippines sought to earn the right to print their own currency.

The correct answer is B:) A three-year fight for Filipino independence in which 4,000 American troops and 500,000 Filipino citizens died.

134) Frank Lloyd Wright was a(n)

A) Musician
B) Architect
C) Politician
D) Artist
E) Both A and C

The correct answer is B:) Architect. Frank Lloyd Wright was an internationally acclaimed architect known for his work to create a distinctly "American" style of architecture. His famous works include Fallingwater and the Imperial Hotel of Tokyo.

135) The Hull House was a famous

A) Slaughterhouse
B) Opera House
C) Museum
D) Settlement house
E) None of the above

The correct answer is D:) Settlement house. Although there were over 400 settlement houses throughout the country, the Hull House in Chicago was the most famous.

136) What was Andrew Carnegie's intention when he said "There is not such a cradle of democracy upon the earth as the Free Public Library, this republic of letters, where neither rank, office, nor wealth receives the slightest consideration."?

A) To support the growth of free public libraries
B) Attempt to support the restriction of libraries to the wealthy
C) Appeal to congress to stop funding public libraries
D) Encourage people in support of republican ideals to write more letters
E) None of the above

The correct answer is A:) To support the growth of free public libraries. Andrew Carnegie was a strong support of public libraries. He felt that knowledge would allow people to improve their situation, no matter what their socio-economic background was.

137) Which of the following cases challenged the practice of fundamentalist teaching in schools?

A) Plessy v. Ferguson
B) Scopes Trial
C) Brown v. Board of Education
D) Mapp v. Ohio
E) None of the above

The correct answer is B:) Scopes Trial. Fundamentalism was the practice of teaching things according to the Bible. A Biology teacher, John Scopes, was sued for teaching evolution, which contrasts with the creation story of the Bible. He was convicted but the event started a shift in opinions away from fundamentalism.

138) Which of the following describes Theodore Roosevelt's foreign policy?

I. Dollar Diplomacy
II. Big Stick Diplomacy
III. Nonviolent Direct Action

A) II only
B) I and II only
C) I and III only
D) II and III only
E) I, II and III only

The correct answer is B:) I and II only. Theodore Roosevelt is famous for saying "speak softly and carry a big stick." This is the origin of Big Stick Diplomacy. His intervention in the Dominican Republic characterized Dollar Diplomacy which was more fully instituted under President Taft.

139) How many African-Americans were registered to vote under the Freedom Summer project?

A) 120
B) 1,200
C) 12,000
D) 102,000
E) 120,000

The correct answer is C:) 12,000.

140) Which president is known for using Bruce Springsteen's song *Born in the USA* as part of their campaign?

   A) Lyndon B. Johnson
   B) George H.W. Bush
   C) Richard Nixon
   D) Ronald Reagan
   E) Jimmy Carter

The correct answer is D:) Ronald Reagan. Reagan's main focus in his campaign was winning over liberal and democratic voters. He hoped that by associating himself with a strong liberal and catchy song he would accomplish this.

141) Who wrote The Jungle?

   A) Mary Elizabeth Clyens
   B) Jack Kerouac
   C) Michael Harrington
   D) Jacob Riis
   E) Upton Sinclair

The correct answer is E:) Upton Sinclair. This 1906 work was about the dirty conditions in meat packing plants.

142) The famous quote "You shall not press down upon the brow of labor this crown of thorns; you shall not crucify mankind upon a cross of gold," was delivered by William Jennings Bryan, former United States Representative from Nebraska, as part of his Cross of Gold speech, and was in support of _____.

   A) The gold standard
   B) Limiting the silver legal tender
   C) Paper money
   D) Bimetallism or "free silver"
   E) None of the above

The correct answer is D:) Bimetallism or "free silver". In 1896, at the Democratic National Convention, William Jennings Bryan argued in support of bimetallism because he felt that producing legal tender out of both gold and silver was necessary to maintain the United States' economic health. The speech was so widely received that it catapulted Bryan into the Democratic nomination for president.

143) In his book The Gospel of Wealth, Andrew Carnegie is quoted as saying, "_____," in relation to his feelings regarding the wealthy and philanthropy.

A) The man who dies thus rich dies disgraced
B) There is little success where there is little laughter
C) The first man gets the oyster, the second man gets the shell
D) As I grow older, I pay less attention to what men say. I just watch what they do
E) None of the above

The correct answer is A:) The man who dies thus rich dies disgraced. The other three quotes are also attributed to Carnegie, but are not found as part of The Gospel of Wealth.

144) During his surrender at the conclusion of the Nez Perce War, Chief Joseph was quoted as saying,

A) "I will tell you in my way how the Indian sees things. The white man has more words to tell you how they look to him, but it does not require many words to speak the truth."
B) "Whenever the white man treats the Indian as they treat each other then we shall have no more wars."
C) "I claim a right to live on my land and accord you the privilege to return to yours."
D) "Hear me, my Chiefs! I am tired; my heart is sick and sad. From where the Sun now stands, I will fight no more forever."
E) None of the above

The correct answer is D:) "Hear me, my Chiefs! I am tired; my heart is sick and sad. From where the Sun now stands, I will fight no more forever." The other three quotes are attributed to Chief Joseph as well, but not following his surrender to General Nelson Appleton Miles.

145) During May 1960, a U-2 spy plane was shot down by the Soviet Air Defense Forces and led to the embarrassment of the United States, since President Dwight D. Eisenhower had given the _____ permission to conduct reconnaissance missions over key Soviet targets. The incident marked further deterioration of relations between the U.S. and the Soviet Union.

   A) National Security Agency
   B) Federal Bureau of Investigation
   C) Central Intelligence Agency
   D) Defense Intelligence Agency
   E) Homeland Security Department

The correct answer is C:) Central Intelligence Agency. Francis Gary Powers, the pilot who was flying at the time, was a CIA employee.

146) Activist Cesar Chávez was known for his nonviolent protests in order to gain better working conditions and wages for _____ workers.

   A) Construction
   B) Coal mine
   C) Postal
   D) Transportation
   E) Farm

The correct answer is E:) Farm. In 1962, Cesar Chávez co-founded the National Farm Workers Association, which sought specifically to bring better conditions to farm workers in California.

147) There were many reasons that African Americans fought in the Spanish-American War, but most specifically they

   A) Wanted revenge for the sinking of the USS Maine
   B) Hoped to gain equal rights in the U.S.
   C) Wanted to protect their Cuban relatives
   D) Wanted a free meal
   E) None of the above

The correct answer is B:) Hoped to gain equal rights in the U.S. Even though the Emancipation Proclamation had been passed several years before the war, African Americans still fought against discrimination. They hoped that by contributing to the Spanish-American War, they would be more fully recognized as citizens of equal status.

148) The Cuban Missile Crisis of 1962 pitted the U.S. against the communist Soviet Union during the height of the Cold War and resulted in

    A) The reconsideration of the nuclear arms race
    B) The Bay of Pigs invasion
    C) The quarantine of Cuba
    D) The Paris Accords
    E) None of the above

The correct answer is A:) The reconsideration of the nuclear arms race. Given the tense environment this incident caused, both the U.S. and the Soviet Union began to reconsider the need for nuclear weapons and they took the first steps to removing nuclear weapons by signing the Nuclear Test Treaty Ban.

149) Most 1950s television programs covered a wide variety of topics, including _____, opposition to the Korean War, and the concept that men worked and women stayed at home.

    A) Women entering the Korean War
    B) Women leaving the Korean War
    C) Men leaving the workforce and working at home
    D) Women leaving the workforce
    E) Women entering the workforce

The correct answer is E:) Women entering the workforce. Since World War II had only ended a few years prior and the Korean War was just ramping up, there were a variety of topics covered during this television decade.

150) Given the following list: Malcolm X assassination, MLK letter, Montgomery Bus Boycott, and the Birmingham campaign, which event was the first to occur?

    A) MLK letter
    B) Montgomery Bus Boycott
    C) Malcolm X assassination
    D) Birmingham campaign
    E) None of the above

The correct answer is B:) Montgomery Bus Boycott. The MLK letter happened in 1963 as did the Birmingham campaign, while the assassination of Malcolm X occurred in 1965. The Montgomery Bus Boycott started in 1955 and ended in 1956.

151) Of the many U.S. controversies over the years, none have been more hotly debated than the Manhattan Project, which led to the development of the atomic bomb near the end of World War II. There are many reasons why historians believe the atomic bomb was employed, including to prevent an invasion by the Japanese mainland and

A) To end the war
B) To prevent the attack on Pearl Harbor
C) To prevent the attack on Midway Island
D) To prevent the siege of Great Britain
E) None of the above

The correct answer is A:) To end the war. All of the other events had already happened at this point.

152) During the early 1980s, U.S. President Ronald Reagan deployed American troops to what country in the hopes of avoiding an Arab-Israeli war in the Middle East?

A) Israel
B) Saudi Arabia
C) Syria
D) Lebanon
E) Turkey

The correct answer is D:) Lebanon. Due to the strategic value of the Sannin ridge, Israeli and Syrian forces clashed in Lebanon. In the hopes of ending the fighting, the U.S. contributed troops to the area to help maintain a ceasefire and oversee the removal of Palestine Liberation Organization (PLO) forces.

153) Following a class reunion, Betty Friedan wrote The Feminine Mystique, whose main theme was about

    A) The unhappiness of men in the 1950s and 1960s due in part to them working long hours outside the home
    B) The unhappiness of men in the 1950s and 1960s due in part to their lack of fulfillment outside the home
    C) The unhappiness of women in the 1950s and 1960s due in part to their lack of fulfillment outside the home
    D) The unhappiness of women in the 1950s and 1960s due in part to them working long hours outside the home
    E) None of the above

The correct answer is C:) The unhappiness of women in the 1950s and 1960s due in part to their lack of fulfillment outside the home. The other answers are variations on the correct answer.

154) _____ was produced by the Ford Motor Company and is regarded as one of first affordable automobiles.

    A) The Model A
    B) The Model T
    C) The Model C
    D) The Model N
    E) The Model S

The correct answer is B:) The Model T. The other answers are variations on the correct answer.

155) The 1920 U.S. census results showed

    A) A decline in the U.S. population
    B) A continuing shift of the U.S. population out of the U.S. to other countries
    C) A continuing shift of the U.S. population out of urban areas to more rural areas
    D) A continuing shift of the U.S. population out of rural areas to more urban areas
    E) None of the above

The correct answer is D:) A continuing shift of the U.S. population out of rural areas to more urban areas. The other answers are variations on the correct answer.

156) President Eisenhower's main reason for wanting to construct an interstate highway system was to

   A) Provide ways for the rural population to reach the urban areas
   B) Transport military supplies throughout the U.S. in case of a foreign invasion
   C) Provide an easy means of traveling across the country
   D) To be remembered in the history books
   E) None of the above

The correct answer is B:) Transport military supplies throughout the U.S. in case of a foreign invasion. Eisenhower had experienced the European highway system and the ease at which it allowed military forces to move about Europe especially during World War II. He felt this was an important aspect to bring to the U.S.

157) The 1928 presidential election was significant because it was the first time a _____ had been nominated as a presidential candidate.

   A) Lutheran
   B) Presbyterian
   C) Roman Catholic
   D) Methodist
   E) Baptist

The correct answer is C:) Roman Catholic. Alfred Smith was nominated by the Democratic candidate in 1928 to campaign against Herbert Hoover since the major issues of the election related to religion and prohibition.

158) The Organization of Petroleum Exporting Countries, or OPEC, was created by five of the world's major oil-exporting countries. They are Iran, Iraq, Kuwait, Saudi Arabia, and

   A) France
   B) Great Britain
   C) Russia
   D) The United States
   E) Venezuela

The correct answer is E:) Venezuela. The other countries are not members of OPEC.

159) The Organization of Petroleum Exporting Countries or OPEC was formed in _____ to coordinate the petroleum policies of contributing members and to provide aid to any participating nations.

A) 1959
B) 1960
C) 1970
D) 1965
E) 1962

The correct answer is B:) 1960. OPEC was created in Baghdad in 1960 by five founding members and is headquartered in Vienna, Austria.

160) _____ is the act of making accusations of treason or subversion without proper evidence and is related to the Second Red Scare of the late 1940s and early 1950s.

A) Cohnism
B) Carterism
C) Trumanism
D) Nixonism
E) McCarthyism

The correct answer is E:) McCarthyism. Following a speech given in February of 1950, Joseph McCarthy claimed to have the names of 205 Communists working in the State Department. McCarthy went on to become a U.S. senator and the term McCarthyism refers to the timeframe in which he accused numerous individuals of being Communist collaborators or spies.

161) The Korean War was sparked when North Korean Communist forces crossed the 38th Parallel into South Korea. In response, U.S. President _____ sent naval ships and air support to aid South Korea.

A) Eisenhower
B) Coolidge
C) Carter
D) Truman
E) None of the above

The correct answer is D:) Truman. Harry S. Truman was president of the U.S. from 1945 to 1953. The Korean War started in 1950, during his term.

162) Following the Second Red Scare, Senator Joseph McCarthy was condemned by the U.S. Senate in relation to his

A) Failure to identify key Soviet sleeper agents
B) Failure to run for office again
C) Failure to properly Mirandize suspected Communist agents
D) Failure to provide concrete evidence of Communist activities within the U.S. government
E) None of the above

The correct answer is D:) Failure to provide concrete evidence of Communist activities within the U.S. government. McCarthy caused such a frenzy surrounding Communist fears that the U.S. Senate formed a special committee and appointed him as the chairman.

163) The _____ was the collection of craft unions founded in 1886 in Columbus, Ohio.

A) American Federation of Labor (AFL)
B) Congress of Industrial Organizations (CIO)
C) Knights of Labor
D) Cigar Maker's International Union
E) Federation of Organized Trades and Labor Unions

The correct answer is A:) American Federation of Labor (AFL). The other four options are various other union groups that were formed either before or after the AFL formation in 1886.

164) Under President Jimmy Carter's guidance, the U.S. foreign policy shifted to a focus on

A) Abandoning the moral U.S. principles in place at the time
B) Adopting the same tactics as our adversaries
C) The highest moral U.S. principles
D) Adopting the same tactics as Vietnam
E) None of the above

The correct answer is C:) The highest moral U.S. principles. President Carter felt that the U.S. foreign policy should reflect U.S. values and not the adoption of foreign nations' flawed policies.

165) President Jimmy Carter sought to quell the economic crisis in the U.S. during the early 1980s by calming inflation rates through the introduction of

    A) High interest rates
    B) Low interest rates
    C) Inflated interest rates
    D) Deflated interest rates
    E) None of the above

The correct answer is A:) High interest rates. The other answers are variations on the correct answer.

166) The Camp David Accords led directly to the 1979 Egypt-_____ Peace Treaty.

    A) Saudi Arabia
    B) Iran
    C) Iraq
    D) Israel
    E) United States

The correct answer is D:) Israel. Following twelve days of secret negotiations at Camp David, overseen by President Jimmy Carter, the Egyptian President Anwar El Sadat and Israeli Prime Minister Menachem Begin agreed on two separate initiatives that worked to improve Israeli-Egyptian relations.

167) The Occupation of Alcatraz centered on the _____ occupation of Alcatraz Island in 1963 and was in response to the Treaty of Fort Laramie that stated all retired and abandoned federal properties were to be returned to these individuals whenever they occupied the abandoned lands.

    A) Native American
    B) African American
    C) Asian American
    D) Spanish American
    E) None of the above

The correct answer is A:) Native American. The Occupation of Alcatraz lasted for nearly two years and was started by 89 American Indians who claimed that the Treaty of Fort Laramie gave them the right to reclaim the land.

168) Following the Enron scandal of 2001, the _____ was passed to provide comprehensive business practices reform that required better oversight into the financial management of large corporations.

   A) Sarbanes-Carter Act
   B) Sarbanes-Truman Act
   C) Washington-Oxley Act
   D) Sarbanes-Oxley Act
   E) None of the above

The correct answer is D:) Sarbanes-Oxley Act. The other three answers are variations on the correct answer.

169) The Ford Motor Company assembly line was one of the first of its kind to use _____ parts and a moving line.

   A) Copper
   B) Nickel
   C) Aluminum
   D) Steel
   E) Interchangeable

The correct answer is E:) Interchangeable. The other answers are materials of parts and do not specifically speak to the uniqueness of the Ford Motor Company assembly line.

170) William Jennings Bryan's _____ speech was in favor of free silver.

   A) Silver Cross
   B) I Have a Dream
   C) Cross of Gold
   D) Inauguration
   E) None of the above

The correct answer is C:) Cross of Gold. William Jennings Bryan was a little known Democratic candidate for the United States presidential election of 1896. His famous "Cross of Gold" speech in favor of using silver as well as gold for minting U.S. currency is widely credited with earning him the Democratic nomination for president.

 # Test Taking Strategies

Here are some test-taking strategies that are specific to this test and to other CLEP tests in general:
- Keep your eyes on the time. Pay attention to how much time you have left.
- Read the entire question and read all the answers. Many questions are not as hard to answer as they may seem. Sometimes, a difficult sounding question really only is asking you how to read an accompanying chart. Chart and graph questions are on most CLEP tests and should be an easy free point.
- If you don't know the answer immediately, the new computer-based testing lets you mark questions and come back to them later if you have time.
- Read the wording carefully. Some words can give you hints to the right answer. There are no exceptions to an answer when there are words in the question such as "always" "all" or "none." If one of the answer choices includes most or some of the right answers, but not all, then that is not the answer. Here is an example:

    The primary colors include all of the following:
    A) Red, Yellow, Blue, Green
    B) Red, Green, Yellow
    C) Red, Orange, Yellow
    D) Red, Yellow, Blue
    E) None of the above

    Although item A includes all the right answers, it also includes an incorrect answer, making it incorrect. If you didn't read it carefully, were in a hurry, or didn't know the material well, you might fall for this.
- Make a guess on a question that you do not know the answer to. There is no enalty for an incorrect answer. Eliminate the answer choices that you know are incorrect. For example, this will let your guess be a 1 in 3 chance instead.

 # What Your Score Means

Based on your score, you may, or may not, qualify for credit at your specific institution. At University of Phoenix, a score of 50 is passing for full credit. At Utah Valley State College, the score is unpublished, the school will accept credit on a case-by-case basis. Another school, Brigham Young University (BYU) does not accept CLEP credit. To find out what score you need for credit, you need to get that information from your school's website or academic advisor.

You can score between 20 and 80 on any CLEP test. Some exams include percentile ranks. Each correct answer is worth one point. You lose no points for unanswered or incorrect questions.

 Test Preparation

How much you need to study depends on your knowledge of a subject area. If you are interested in literature, took it in school, or enjoy reading then your studying and preparation for the literature or humanities test will not need to be as intensive as someone who is new to literature.

This book is much different than the regular CLEP study guides. This book actually teaches you the information that you need to know to pass the test. If you are particularly interested in an area, or you want more information, do a quick search online. We've tried not to include too much depth in areas that are not as essential on the test. Everything in this book will be on the test. It is important to understand all major theories and concepts listed in the table of contents. It is also very important to know any bolded words.

Don't worry if you do not understand or know a lot about the area. With minimal study, you can complete and pass the test.

 Legal Note

All rights reserved. This Study Guide, Book and Flashcards are protected under U.S. Copyright Law. No part of this book or study guide or flashcards may be reproduced, distributed or stored in a retrieval system, or transmitted in any form or by any means, electronic, mechanical, photocopying, recording, or otherwise, without the prior written permission of the publisher Breely, Crush & Associates LLC. This manual is not supported by or affiliated with the College Board, creators of the CLEP test. CLEP is a registered trademark of the College Entrance Examination Board, which does not endorse this book.

FLASHCARDS

This section contains flashcards for you to use to further your understanding of the material and test yourself on important concepts, names or dates. Read the term or question then flip the page over to check the answer on the back. Keep in mind that this information may not be covered in the text of the study guide. Take your time to study the flashcards, you will need to know and understand these concepts to pass the test.

Neutral in Both Thought and Deed	**First U.S. College**
World War 2 established the U.S. as what?	**Anti-Masons**
Liberty Party	**Masons**
American Party	**Greenback Party**

Harvard	Woodrow Wilson
Anti Mason party	A Super Power
Fraternal order	Anti-slavery party
Wanted paper currency	Know-Nothing-Party

Populist Party	**Socialist Party**
Eugene Debs	**Progressive Party**
Who said, "The best system is to have one party to govern and the other party to watch"?	OASDI is what?
What are the 5 main public assistance programs?	Who said we have the right to "Life, liberty and the pursuit of happiness"?

Believes in equal disbursement of resources	People's Party
Includes three different parties: Bull Moose Party, League for Progressive Political Action, The Election of 1948	Launched Socialist Party
Old Age, Survivors, Disability Insurance - also known as Social Security	Thomas Reed
John Locke	Medicaid, SSI, AFDC, Food Stamps, Public Housing

What is the firstamendment?	Who said "give me liberty or give me death"?
Townsend Duties were placed on what items?	James Madison made which treaty?
What was the first nuclear powered submarine named?	Which President served a third term?
Panama Canal shortened sailing time between which two American cities?	Green Revolution

Patrick Henry	Church and State
Treaty of Ghent	Glass, lead, paint, paper and imported tea
Franklin Delano Roosevelt	Nautilus
A time when there was a significant increase of agricultural products - 20th century	New York and San Francisco

Grapes of Wrath took place during which era?	Anthropology
Reconstruction	Samuel Gompers
2nd Amendment	3rd Amendment
6th Amendment	4th Amendment

The study of all human life aspects and culture	The Great Depression
"Pure and simple unionism"	Rebuilding after the American Civil War
No quartering	Right to Bear Arms
No unreasonable search and seizures	Right to a speedy trial

20th Amendment	**Atlanta Compromise**
Big Stick Diplomacy	**Populism**
19th Amendment	**Brown v. Board of Education**
Compromise of 1877	**Marshall Plan**

A speech by Booker T. Washington in which he encouraged education as a method of social advancement.	Passed in 1932. Defined the term end date for the President, Vice President, and representatives in Congress.
A belief supported mainly by farmers favoring coinage of silver and paper money regulation of railroads, national income tax, and government help for farmers.	A foreign policy based on Roosevelt's saying "speak softly and carry a big stick" which relied on military intimidation.
1954. The Supreme Court declared that segregation in public schools was unconstitutional.	Passed in 1919. Gave women the right to vote.
A large scale economic project which involved strengthening economic foundations in European countries as a method of combating the spread of communism.	Also known as the "Corrupt Bargain," this compromise allowed Rutherford B Hayes to be pronounced President after a disputed election based on the unwritten deal that he would move troops out of the South.

Cuban Missile Crisis	**NAACP**
Fourteen Points	**Scopes trial**
George Wallace	**Sherman Antitrust Act**
Gilded Age	**Harlem Renaissance**

National Association for the Advancement of Colored People. A group which worked for to gain equal treatment and rights for colored people.

In October 1962 the US discovered that Russia was building nuclear missile launch sites in Cuba the two countries were brought to the brink of nuclear war, luckily Russia agreed to dismantle the sites.

Biology teacher John Scopes was sued for illegally teaching evolution. He was convicted but the event started a shift in opinions away from fundamentalism.

Wilson's contribution to the Versailles treaty ending WWI. They included freedom of the seas and the League of Nations.

An attempt to control the development of monopolies harmful to the economy. The act essentially made purposely creating a monopoly illegal.

The first candidate torun under the American Independent Party in 1968 who was popular in the South and among blue collar workers.

A literary movement headed by black writers in the 1920s and centered in Harlem, New York.

A term used to describe a period of great economic growth and perceived prosperity created by industrialization in the late 1800s. While some people became very rich there was a high poverty rate and government corruption.

13th Amendment	**Haymarket Affair**
Hiroshima	**Homestead Act**
15th Amendment	**Jim Crow Laws**
16th Amendment	**Ku Klux Klan**

A workers riot in Chicago in which a number of police and citizens died.	Passed in 1865. Officiallyended slavery in the United States.
Offered free land in the West to encouraged immigration.	The site of the first atomicbomb after Japan refused to surrender in WWII.
The name for laws passed in the South after the Civil War which promoted segregation and racism. Also called black codes.	Passed in 1869. Guaranteed citizens the right to vote regardless of race.
A white supremacist group formed after the Civil War which terrorized blacks. It was disbanded in 1869 but resurfaced in the early 1900s.	Passed in 1909. Allows Congress to levy income taxes.

Lusitania	**Social Darwinism**
Martin Luther King Jr.	**Monroe Doctrine**
Red Scare	**New Deal**
New Federalism	**17th Amendment**

A belief derived from Darwin's theories in which people believed that the poor were poor because they were inferior to the rich.

A British passenger ship which was sunk by German submarines. Because there were many Americans on board, it increased support for entering WWI.

A statement issued by President Monroe which forbade further colonization of the Western hemisphere by European countries.

A Baptist minister and famous leader of the civil rights movement in the mid 1900s whose ideas focused on a theory of nonviolence.

FDRs plan to bring immediate relief to the economy, and eventually stabilize it.

When the Communist Party began gaining strength in the United States, it caused a panic resulting in the Palmer Raids. Over 4,000 suspected (unverified) Communists were jailed or deported.

Passed in 1912. Modified the Constitution to allow people to elect Senators, where originally they had been chosen by state legislatures.

Nixon's slogan for returning power and resources to states and people.

Crime of 1873	**New Immigration**
New Nationalism	**Pearl Harbor**
Plessy v. Ferguson	**Booker T. Washington**
Dollar Diplomacy	**Progressive Party**

A major wave of immigrants from 1865-1910 consisting primarily of immigrants from Southern and Eastern Europe.	Name given to the Coinage Law of 1873 by those who opposed it. The law removed silver from circulation as money.
An attack on a United States Pacific Fleet in which 18 ships and 200 aircraft were destroyed, killing 3000 people. The event caused the United States to declare war on Japan.	Roosevelt's philosophy that a strong national government should protect the underprivileged and promote social justice.
An influential black speaker and leader of the late 1800s. Famous for his Atlanta Compromise speech.	1896. The Supreme Court ruled that states have the right to enforce segregation in schools on the basis of "separate but equal" doctrine.
Formed in the 1890s. Attacked monopolies and supported government regulations in areas such as transportation and labor.	A foreign policy meant to avoid war by giving foreign countries financial aid and strengthening their economies.

Quarantine Speech	**Radical Republicans**
Robert LaFollete	**Roosevelt Corollary**
15th Amendment	**Grandfather clause**
18th Amendment	**Social Gospel Movement**

Believed that Lincoln had been too compassionate, and wanted to punish the South after the Civil War. 	Speech in which FDR spoke out against fascism and compared it to a contagious disease that should be quarantined. 
An addition to the Monroe Doctrine which stated that the United States would intervene to maintain stability in South American countries. 	A famous debater and leader of the Progressive movement. 
One type of Jim Crow law which kept black people from voting by allowing a person to vote only if their grandfather could. 	Passed in 1869. Guaranteed citizens the right to vote regardless of race. 
A movement of the late 1800s to early 1900s which emphasized social responsibility and charity. 	Passed in 1917. Made the manufacturing and sale of alcohol illegal. 

Spanish War	Square Deal
Tenements	Thurgood Marshall
Truman Doctrine	W.E.B. Dubois
Zimmerman Telegram	14th Amendment

Roosevelt's term for his intention to protect the rights of the working class.	Resulted in United States control of Puerto Rico, the Philippines, Guam and Cuba. The war ended Spanish involvement in the Americas.
Head Lawyer in the Brown v. Board of Education case, and later the first black Supreme Court Justice.	Poorly constructed and overcrowded housing for poor urban workers.
Founder of the NAACP who held a militant opinion about race relations.	President Truman's policy which stated that the United States would offer financial and military support to countries in an effort to stop the spread of Communism.
Passed in 1866. Ensured due process and equal protection under the law, defined citizenship and declared that the US government would not pay compensation for freed slaves.	A message sent from Germany to Mexico, requesting an alliance against the United States. The message was intercepted and increased support for WWI.

www.ingramcontent.com/pod-product-compliance
Lightning Source LLC
Chambersburg PA
CBHW081829300426
44116CB00014B/2525